The **ESSEN**

Data
Structures I

Rev. Dennis C. Smolarski, S.J., Ph.D.
Associate Professor of Mathematics
Santa Clara University, CA

> This book covers the usual course outline of Data
> Structures I. For related topics, see *"THE
> ESSENTIALS OF DATA STRUCTURES II."*

 Research & Education Association
61 Ethel Road West
Piscataway, New Jersey 08854

THE ESSENTIALS®
OF DATA STRUCTURES I

Printed in the United States of America

Library of Congress Control Number 00-132041

International Standard Book Number 0-87891-728-4

ESSENTIALS is a registered trademark of
Research & Education Association, Piscataway, New Jersey 08854

WHAT "THE ESSENTIALS" WILL DO FOR YOU

This book is a review and study guide. It is comprehensive and it is concise.

It helps in preparing for exams and in doing homework, and remains a handy reference source at all times.

It condenses the vast amount of detail characteristic of the subject matter and summarizes the **essentials** of the field.

It will thus save hours of research and preparation time.

The book provides quick access to the important facts, principles, procedures, and techniques in the field.

Materials needed for exams can be reviewed in summary form – eliminating the need to read and re-read many pages of textbook and class notes. The summaries will even tend to bring detail to mind that had been previously read or noted.

This "ESSENTIALS" book has been prepared by experts in the field, and has been carefully reviewed to ensure its accuracy and maximum usefulness.

Dr. Max Fogiel
Program Director

CONTENTS

CHAPTER 1

INTRODUCTION

1.1 DATA AND PROGRAMS

All computer programs involve information or **data**. A program is of little use if there is no information produced at the end of its execution. Some programs merely *generate* data, such as a program to generate prime numbers. These types of programs usually do not require any input data, but merely create the information desired by the programmer. Other programs *process* input data and create more data as a result, such as bookkeeping and billing programs that examine files of charges and then generate bills to be mailed to customers. Whether a program needs input data or not, it nonetheless needs to *store* some data, which is then used to generate other data desired by the programmer.

The study of *data structures* is a study of the possible ways of organizing and storing information; that is, a study of the various ways to *structure data*, and a study of the way that some data is related to other data. Depending on the way data

1

is arranged ("structured"), computer operations involving that data may become less or more efficient, or less or more complex operations such as information retrieval and modification.

A study of data structures usually involves examining the operations, programs or algorithms associated with the various structures, although a detailed analysis of these algorithms is normally part of a separate field of study, usually called the *Theory of Algorithms*. In general, good algorithms lead to good programs. But the efficiency of programs can be improved by an intelligent and prudent choice of the data structures used to store the needed information.

1.2 ABSTRACT DATA TYPES

Certain data structures (e.g., scalar data — Chapter 2, and arrays — Chapter 3) are built into every computer language. However, not every language has the full range of the more complex structures (e.g., pointer variables frequently used in linked lists — Chapter 6). To overcome some of the difficulty encountered when converting from one language to another and also to allow for improvement in the internal implementation of more complex structures in various versions of a program, certain data structures are now commonly termed **Abstract Data Types**.

An **Abstract Data Type** (abbreviated as ADT) is any unit of data (usually complex) not built into a specific programming language. For example, the structure *stack* (see Chapter 7) can be called an ADT since most languages do not contain "stack" as an elementary data type or structure. In a data-base management program, the *database* might be considered an ADT.

Once an ADT has been identified, operations can be associated with the ADT (such as insertion, deletion, searching, test-

2

ing whether empty, etc.), and specifications can be drawn up detailing what the ADT contains, and what each operation does.

In many computer languages, a given ADT (such as a stack) may be implemented in several different ways, using different possible fundamental data types and structures. In some languages (such as Modula-2 and Ada), it may even be impossible for someone to know how such an ADT is actually implemented, particularly if the program segment containing the definition of the ADT and its operations was written by another programmer.

ADTs provide a beneficial distinction between *external representation* of data structures along with their related operations, and the actual *internal implementation*. This distinction becomes particularly useful in larger programs. If the modifications of ADTs are done only by using carefully written operations, then fewer errors usually occur. If a more efficient method to implement an ADT is developed, in a carefully written program the sections defining the ADT and its operations can be replaced by the newer code without affecting the other segments of the program. A programming team can determine which ADTs will be used, how the related operations are to work, and what the external specifications should be, thus leaving the actual internal implementation to someone else. As long as users follow the external specifications, they should not need to know anything about the internal implementation. The ADT can form a protective fence around the internal implementation both to guard the data structure and also to allow it to be improved without disturbing the rest of the program.

Some of the more complex data structures are frequently described as ADTs. Sometimes several implementations are discussed in detail (as in the case of stacks). Other times, implementations are not discussed at all or only one brief example is given (as in the case of trees). However, programming with ADTs has become a more and more important part of the contemporary study of Data Structures, even though they are not always explicitly mentioned.

1.3 COMMENTS ON TOPICS

The topics covered in this booklet are primarily those recommended for a second course in Computer Science for Computer Science majors, topics listed in the most recent *Association for Computing Machinery* (ACM) curriculum guidelines for course CS2 (as revised in 1984). Some topics, however, may be covered in other courses. For example, topics in Chapters 1 through 6 may sometimes be covered in a first course in Computer Science (ACM course CS1), topics in Chapter 2 sometimes in a course in computer organization (ACM course CS4), and topics in Chapters 11 through 14 (found in *The Essentials of Data Structures II*) sometimes in an intermediate course in data structures (AM course CS7).

In addition, several appendices contain information that, although not intrinsically part of the subject of data structures, are frequently included in data structures texts or are taught in prerequisite courses. This information has been placed in the appendices as a handy reference.

CHAPTER 2

SCALAR VARIABLES

2.1 COMPUTER MEMORY

Computer memory can be envisioned as a huge collection of locations that can store information or data, similar to the banks of post office boxes in a post office. Each individual memory location consists of a number of two-valued (i.e., binary) information storage units. Each of these two-valued storage units is usually called a **bit** (for "*b*inary dig*it*"), and stores a value of 0 or 1 (or "off" or "on"). Each memory location has a unique address so information can be stored and retrieved easily, and the addresses are usually numbered sequentially (often starting at 0). Thus if a small computer has 256,000 memory locations, they are sequentially numbered from 0 to 255,999.

A standard memory location on a mainframe computer is traditionally called a **word** and typically consists of 8, 16, 32, 36, 40, or 60 bits. An (addressable) subsection of a word is called a **byte** and is commonly used to represent an encoded character. A byte usually consists of 8 bits, even though only 7 may be used to represent a character in code. On occasion, a half of a byte is called a **nibble**.

Larger computers (i.e., "mainframes") usually have a

longer word size, and these words can sometimes be subdivided. In most personal computers, memory is usually arranged in bytes, which are joined together if needed for larger data.

2.2 DATA TYPES

In most contemporary programming languages, there are at least four standard *types*:

INTEGER	(i.e., whole numbers such as 2, 34, – 234),
REAL	(i.e., numbers that can contain a decimal point),
CHARACTER	(i.e., letters, symbols, and numbers stored as characters),
BOOLEAN	(i.e., values related to two-valued logic, sometimes called **LOGICAL**).

Any unit of information that is used in a program must be classified according to one of the allowable types and in most languages this classification cannot be changed during the course of the program's execution.

Information stored in memory is also classified as to whether it remains constant throughout the program (such as 3.1415926) or whether the contents of that memory location are allowed to be changed. Memory locations that contain unchangeable data are called **constants**. Memory locations that contain changeable data are called **variables**.

Since computer memory can only store binary information, all information, numeric or non-numeric, has to be translated into some sort of binary code before storage. The code must be unique as to *type* and easy to use in operations. In addition, there should be some way of determining what type of information is stored in which memory location, so that the information can be interpreted correctly.

6

To aid the computer in determining what type of information is stored where, when a program is compiled, a **symbol table** is created in which each variable is listed along with its *type*. Normally, other information is also stored in a symbol table, especially the variable's memory location, and any initial value.

A constant or variable is called **scalar** (or *simple*) if it is associated with *one* memory location.

2.3   ENCODING DATA

2.3.1   INTEGERS

In the binary representation of integers, the left-most bit is interpreted as a **sign bit**, which is 0 for positive numbers and 1 for negative numbers. The other bits store the **magnitude** of the number (sometimes called the *mantissa*). This magnitude is interpreted in different ways depending on whether the number is positive or negative and depending on which method is used by the computer for representing signed integers.

There are *three* common schemes used to store signed integers. The actual method employed depends on the computer being used and each computer employs only one scheme.

Positive integers are encoded in direct binary notation no matter which of the three schemes is used, e.g.,

$$2_{10} = 00...00010_2$$
$$9_{10} = 00...01001_2$$

Negative integers are encoded differently according to the rules of the scheme being used.

a) **Sign Magnitude** — The first bit indicates the *sign*, and the other bits indicate the number in standard (i.e., positive = "magnitude") form. E.g.,

$$2_{10} = 00...00010_2$$
$$-2_{10} = 10...00010_2$$

PROBLEMS
In this scheme, there exists one representation for +0 (= 00...000) and a different one for − 0 (= 10...000). Arithmetic (with positive and negative numbers) is difficult, since it must first be determined whether both numbers are of the same or of different signs, and then the appropriate algorithm used.

b) **One's Complement** — The first bit indicates the sign, but all other bits are (one's) complements of the positive number representation. In other words, a 1 bit turns into a 0 bit and a 0 bit turns into a 1. E.g.,

$$2_{10} = 00...00010_2$$
$$-2_{10} = 11...11101_2$$

PROBLEM
In this scheme, there (also) exist two different representations for +0 (= 00...000) and − 0 (=11...111). However, here the arithmetic is easy. The same algorithm is used no matter what the signs of the two numbers are.

c) **Two's Complement** — First bit (also) indicates the sign, but the other bits are derived by first complementing the positive number representation and then adding 1 (i.e., adding 1 to the 1's complement representation). E.g.,

$$2_{10} = 00...00010_2$$
$$-2_{10} = 11...11110_2$$

8

Note: in this scheme, there is only *one* representation for 0, and the arithmetic is also fairly easy.

Comment: Technically, the three schemes of sign-magnitude, one's complement and two's complement are applicable to *all* signed integers, *both* positive and negative. However, there is *no difference in the resulting coded number for positive numbers*. Only when encoding and decoding *negative* numbers must the scheme be known in order to perform the coding correctly.

2.3.2 REAL NUMBERS

Real numbers are stored in two sections in one word using a format related to the so-called "scientific notation." A real number expressed in scientific notation is written with a section containing the decimal point (usually called the **mantissa** or the *significant digits*), multiplied by 10 raised to some power (called the *exponent*). For example, one million (1,000,000) can be written as 1.0×10^6 or as 100.0×10^4. When real numbers are stored in a computer, the mantissa is *normalized* (i.e., usually there are no digits to the left of the decimal point and no leading zeroes to the right of the decimal point). E.g.,

$0.0025 \Rightarrow$	$.25 \times 10^{-2}$	$\Rightarrow$ often written .25E−2
$3000.0 \Rightarrow$	$.30 \times 10^4$	$\Rightarrow$ often written .30E+4

Whether the "binary" point is assumed *before* or *after* the digits of the mantissa varies with the system. The point itself is never stored.

Thus, for any real number, a total of four units of information must be stored in a word: the binary version of the mantissa, the sign of the mantissa, the binary version of the expo-

9

nent, and the sign of the exponent. Note that as seen in the example above, the sign of the exponent can be negative while the sign of the mantissa can be positive!

For purpose of example, assume that a computer has a 40 bit word. One possible way in which the bits of a word are used for storing a real number might be the following:

Exp Sign	Exponent	Mant Sign	Mantissa
1	6 bits	1	32 bits

It should be noted that *real number arithmetic is more difficult* than integer arithmetic. A simple arithmetic example will illustrate the problem and sketch the steps a computer takes.

EXAMPLE

How are the following numbers added: 0.25E−2 and 0.30E+4? (One cannot merely add the mantissas and the exponents!)

1st: shift the decimal (or binary) point of one number (adjusting both the mantissa and exponent) until *the exponents of both numbers are equal.* E.g.,

.25E−2 ⇒ .00000025E+4

2nd: add the mantissas only. Note that on computers, the limited machine accuracy means that one number may not change the other number, i.e., the sum may actually equal one of the two addends! In our example, the sum would be 0.30000025E+4.

3rd: normalize the computed sum (if necessary). On a computer, after normalization, the number from the computational register is

10

stored in memory, truncating low order bits if necessary. If only six decimal digits can be stored, the stored sum would be the same as one of the two original numbers, i.e., 0.300000E+4.

2.3.3 CHARACTERS

Characters are stored via a coding scheme. Each character, whether it is a letter of the alphabet (upper case or lower case), a digit, or a special symbol (printable or non-printing), is assigned a number in the coding scheme, often called the *collating sequence* (especially when the characters are listed in the numerical order of the code numbers). There are two major schemes in use.

EBCDIC (pronounced "eb-see-dick") is a scheme produced by IBM. It is an acronym for Extended Binary Coded Decimal Information Code, and is still used in some IBM mainframes. This coding is such that the small letters come before the capital letters, which come before the numbers in the collating sequence.

ASCII (pronounced "as-key") is an acronym for American Standard Code for Information Interchange. This is a national standard, in use on most mainframes other than IBM and on most personal computers (including IBM). This coding is such that numbers come before capital letters, which come before small letters in the collating sequence.

2.4 COMMENTS ON VARIABLE TYPES

Programs and computers need to store data correctly in order to use it properly. A program cannot use characters as if they were integers. A computer cannot add reals as it adds integers. The same sequence of bits can mean one thing as a code for a character, something else if it were an integer, and something else if it were a real number. Thus, for most languages it is necessary for the compiler to produce a symbol table, and to distinguish between the various types of simple data stored.

When a unit of data is changed from one type to another, the process is usually called *type conversion*. Even the evaluation of a simple arithmetic expression may involve significant data type conversion that is unknown and invisible to most users. Most languages provide for automatic type conversion between integers and reals when both types of data are involved in a single expression. Since reals cannot be added as if they were integers and vice versa, if both occur in an arithmetic expression, usually the integers are copied to temporary storage locations and converted to reals. Only then is the expression evaluated using real arithmetic alone. FORTRAN includes explicit library functions that enable a user to control conversion between the various numeric data types (i.e., integer, real, double precision, and complex). Real numbers are usually converted to integers by means of an explicit function that either truncates the fractional part of a number or rounds it to the closest integer.

2.5   DECLARING SCALAR VARIABLES

In some languages (e.g, BASIC, FORTRAN, LISP), scalar variables need *not* be declared. However, undeclared variables can lead to problems.

In FORTRAN, if variables are *not* declared, they are given a *default type* based on the first letter: if the initial letter is between I and N (inclusive), the variable is assumed to be of type *integer*. Otherwise, it is of type *real*. To change the default typing (and as good standard programming practice), one uses a type declaration statement.

In other languages (e.g. Pascal, Ada, C, Modula-2), all variables *must* be declared and given a type before use. This is usually done in the variable declaration section before the body of the program code.

CHAPTER 3

ARRAYS AND RECORDS

3.1 AGGREGATE STRUCTURES

Scalar variables do not fill all needs. There are many situations that demand that many scalar variables be associated together. A structure of several memory locations that together form one data structure is often termed an **aggregate structure**. The structure usually is given only one variable name, even though composed of many memory locations. Two of the simplest aggregate structures are *arrays* and *records*.

3.2 ONE-DIMENSION ARRAYS

In general, an **array** is homogeneous data structure with multiple dimensions. In this context, **homogeneous** means that all the elements of the array are of the same data type. Each dimension can be arbitrary in size, but once the sizes of the various dimensions of an array have been determined, in most languages they are fixed for the duration of the program. The memory locations in an array are *sequential* and *consecutive*, like items (e.g., songs) on a magnetic tape cassette. Every array has one name by which it is identified, but the individual elements in an array are accessed by means of one or more subscripts (like the components of a mathematical **vector** or **matrix**). For example, vector **a** of dimension 4 has components a_i where i ranges from 1 to 4.

A one-dimension array is the simplest non-scalar data structure, and its structure and use is similar to that of a mathematical **vector**.

In computer languages, array subscripts are indicated by being enclosed in a pair of parentheses or a pair of square brackets, depending on the rules of the language. For example, the ith element in the array A would be indicated as $A[i]$ in Pascal and $A(I)$ in FORTRAN.

Information in an array is accessed directly and randomly. Thus, an array is sometimes termed a **random access** structure. Some of the items in the structure do not have to be accessed first in order to get to others.

3.3   STORAGE OF ARRAYS

Besides the data stored in the elements of an array, each array also has associated information stored. For each array, a **base location** is stored and, frequently, other information (depending on the language and compiler) such as the number of subscripts (i.e., dimensions), and the maximum/minimum values of each subscript. The **base location** indicates the memory location of the **base**, i.e., the first element of the array.

The locations of the elements of an array are never all stored. The memory location of any element is computed when needed using the base location and the element's subscript(s), as seen in this example.

15

	mem. loc.	

Suppose A(1) was stored at memory location 253.

base (A) = location of 1st element of array A = 253

mem. loc.		
253		A(1)
254		A(2)
255		A(3)
256		...
...		...
...		...

Under the assumption that array elements are stored consecutively, A(2) is located in the first (=2–1) place after A(1). Similarly, A(5) is the fourth (=5–1) element after A(1).

$$\text{location (A(5))} = \text{base (A)} + 5 - 1$$
$$= 253 + 5 - 1 = 257$$

In general,

$$\text{location (A(N))} = \text{base (A)} + N - 1.$$

For some languages and in some implementations, the relevant information for arrays is stored in memory before the data contained in the array, and only the base location is stored in a symbol table. This collection of array information is commonly called the **dope vector** (or **dummy vector**). When used, the base location found in the symbol table sometimes gives the address of the first element of the dope vector rather than the first element in the array. The dope vector in these cases contains the location of the first element of the data.

3.4 TWO- AND HIGHER-DIMENSION ARRAYS

For many problems, one-dimension arrays do not suffice and so two- or higher-dimension arrays must be used. Two-dimension arrays are frequently thought of as representing a table (with rows and columns), and three-dimension arrays as a box with multiple storage compartments (with levels, rows, and columns). The individual storage cells are accessed as in the one-dimension case, via subscripts. With two-dimension arrays, the same convention is followed as with mathematical matrices, in that the first subscript indicates the row, and the second the column. There is no universal agreement on the interpretation of the different subscripts for three- or higher-dimensions.

Any array of any dimension is a data structure with one name for many memory locations. The number of total cells in the array can be calculated by examining the maximum number of each dimension. For example, a two-dimension array A with first element $A(1,1)$ and last element $A(3,5)$ has $3 \times 5 = 15$ total cells for storage. Similarly, a three-dimension array B with first element $B(1,1,1)$ and last element $B(3,2,4)$ has $3 \times 2 \times 4 = 24$ total cells for storage.

As mentioned above, computer memory is numbered sequentially (i.e., linearly), like the inch counter on a tape recorder. Given this fact, the question of how to store a two- or higher-dimension array in a linear computer memory must be discussed.

Storage of a multi-dimension array is done by decomposing the array into subsections, each of which is in some sense linear, and then storing all the subsections in some sort of order. For two-dimension arrays (i.e., matrices or tables), there are two choices for the decomposition:

     — by rows (called "row-major order")
     — by columns (called "column-major order").

In other words, one can imagine taking a (two-dimension) table or matrix printed on a piece of paper and cutting it into strips by rows or by columns. These paper strips can then be fastened together in some order (the first row or column followed by the second, followed by the third and so on) to form one long linear list of data from something that was originally a two-dimension structure.

Knowledge of the storage order is necessary in order to determine which memory location contains which array cell, and different computer languages use different schemes. For example, FORTRAN stores its two dimension arrays by columns, and Pascal stores them by rows.

To determine where a particular element of a two-dimension array is in memory, both the base location and at least one dimension (either row or column depending on the storage scheme of the language) must be known.

To derive a formula associated with a language that uses the column-major order, like FORTRAN, how many elements are in each column (i.e., the number of *rows*) must be known. This information is available to the compiler since it can be derived from the *first* subscript in the array declaration statement.

Suppose a real array A with three rows and five columns is given. In other words, A has been declared as $A(3,5)$ in FORTRAN. Suppose base(A) is 130, in other words, suppose $A(1,1)$ is stored in memory location 130. Where is $A(2,3)$ stored?

Before answering this question, a couple of other questions should be considered first.

Assuming a language that uses column-major order, and given that $A(1,1)$ is stored in 130, what element of the array is stored in memory location 131 (i.e., what is stored right after

$A(1,1)$)? The answer to this question is $A(2,1)$. This element is the second element in the first *column* of the two-dimension array, and thus is stored next to $A(1,1)$.

Where is $A(1,2)$ stored? This is the first element of the second column and it should be stored right after the last element of the first column, i.e., right after $A(3,1)$. $A(3,1)$ is stored in base(A) + **3** (the number of elements per column) − 1 (correction factor because base(A) contains the first element) = 130 + 3 − 1 = 132. Therefore, the answer is that $A(1,2)$ is in the next location after $A(3,1)$, 130 + 3 − 1 + 1 = **133**.

For this array, the following standard two-dimension visualization can be used:

1,1	1,2	1,3	1,4	1,5
130	133	136	139	142
2,1	2,2	2,3	2,4	2,5
131	134	137	140	143
3,1	3,2	3,3	3,4	3,5
132	135	138	141	144

An arbitrary element $A(I, J)$ is stored in base(A) + **3** *(J − 1) + I − 1 (where 3 is the length of the column).

Therefore, $A(2,3)$ is in
$$130 + 3(3-1) + 2 - 1$$
$$= 130 + 3(2) + 2 - 1$$
$$= 130 + 6 + 2 - 1$$
$$= 138 \qquad -1 = 137$$

Another rule is often used to determine a storage location. It is based on the fact that with column-major storage, if the elements of the array are listed in the order in which they are

19

stored in memory, then the *first* subscript varies the fastest. This rule holds also for three- and higher-dimension arrays as well. In the example given above, the elements are stored in the following order (subscripts only): 1,1; 2,1; 3,1; 1,2; 2,2; 3,2; 1,3; 2,3; 3,3; 1,4; 2,4; 3,4; 1,5; 2,5; 3,5. Notice that the first subscript is always changing.

In a language that uses row-major storage (like Pascal) the basic theory for deriving a formula to determine the storage location of an element in the array is the same as above, except that in this case, the number of elements in each *row* needs to be known.

Similarly, there is an easy to remember rule to determine storage locations for arrays stored in row-major order. If the elements of the array are listed in the order in which they are stored in memory, the *last* subscript varies the fastest.

3.5 DECLARING ARRAYS

In general, arrays must be declared before use. They are declared along with their dimensions and the sizes of each dimension. In some languages that allow the definition of new types (e.g., Pascal), rules of style suggest that arrays of a given dimension and size be defined as a new type and given a unique name, and then variables of that new array type can be declared in the variable section. Some languages permit the use of characters as subscripts and some languages permit the initial subscript to be something other than 1 (as in BASIC) or 0 (as in C).

3.6 RECORDS

A two-dimension array is sometimes used to store associated units of information. For example, one row may all refer to information associated with a single person, and each col-

20

umn may refer to a specific category of information for each person, e.g., the first column may always indicate bank balance, the second the account number, etc.

If an array is arranged in this way, each row is called a **record**, i.e., a number of discrete units of information all associated together. Each subsection of a record is called a *field*.

The problem with using an array to store records of information is that an array is a homogeneous structure, i.e., all the units of information in an array must be of the same *type* (e.g., all integers, all reals, all characters, etc.). Therefore, one cannot store a name (an array of *characters*) with an *integer* account number, with a balance (a *real* number).

In some languages (such as C or Pascal), a new **record** type of variable can be defined, and individual variables and arrays can then be declared to be of this new (user-defined) type. (In C, these are called *structures*.) Each of the fields in a record can be of its own type without any restrictions. Thus a record is a heterogeneous aggregate of data structure. It is of fixed-sized, however, once a specific record type has been defined.

For example, in Pascal a new **record** type can be defined for use in storing information for an address label and this new type can be given the name "addressline." After defining the type "addressline," scalar variables and arrays can be declared to be of this type.

```
TYPE addressline   = RECORD
            name    : ARRAY[1...30] OF CHAR;
            street  : ARRAY[1...30] OF CHAR;
            city    : ARRAY[1...30] OF CHAR;
            state   : ARRAY[1...2] OF CHAR;
            zip     : INTEGER
      END;
```

```
VAR        students : ARRAY[1...100] OF addressline;
           line     : addressline;
```

In most languages, both the record variable name and also the specific field are indicated together to specify a particular cell. Pascal uses a period to unite these two identifiers. For example, *line.zip* indicates the *zip* field of the record variable *line*. Also, *students[24].name[1]* indicates the first character of the *name* field of the 24th element in the array *students* (each element of which is a record variable). *students[5]* would indicate the fifth variable in the *students* array, each of which is a complete record variable. Thus, *students[5]* would indicate all five fields together.

As with arrays, all the data associated with a record variable are stored in adjacent memory locations. Thus, in the example given above, the *name* field is stored next to the *street* field and so on. In each field, the normal rules for storage apply. Thus, in the array *students* given above, the *name* field of *students[1]* is separated from the *name* field of *students[2]*, but is adjacent to the *street* field of *student[1]*.

It should also be noted that the declaration used above can hide the true size of a variable that contains records. *students* is an array of 100 elements, but since each element is a record variable of type *addressline*, it contains several parts, most of which are arrays. Each individual variable of type *addressline* consists of 93 independent memory locations (assuming one memory location for each character and integer variable). Thus the array *students* uses 9300 memory locations.

CHAPTER 4

ELEMENTARY SORTING

4.1 SORTING ALGORITHMS

One common operation performed on arrays is **sorting** the array elements, i.e., putting them in some kind of order.

There are a number of different approaches to sorting. The usual problems associated with any algorithm affect these various approaches. The less complicated (and easier to understand) methods are also less efficient, while the more efficient methods are usually more complicated (and difficult to understand).

This chapter will examine two straightforward sorting algorithms that can be used with one-dimension arrays. They are also inefficient. However, more efficient methods appear later (in Chapter 11) after the discussion of more complex data structures.

There are two major elementary approaches to sorting:

a) **Exchange Sorts**: These methods *exchange adjacent* items in an array. The best known exchange sort is **bubble sort**.

b) **Selection Sorts**: These methods search for the next desired item, *select* it, and put it in its proper place in the array.

4.2   BUBBLE SORT

The most common example of an exchange sort is the algorithm known as *bubble sort*. This name is derived from comparing the operation of the algorithm to air bubbles going up slowly in a glass of carbonated water. The bubbles move up bumping other bubbles that get bigger and go up faster. Thus, the lightest bubbles get to the top faster than the others.

The basic principle underlying this algorithm is simple:

— examine adjacent items in an array pair by pair;

— if they are out of order, exchange them.

The algorithm consists of repeatingly performing *passes* on the array, each time applying the basic principle until the array is sorted.

Analyzing the action of the algorithm shows that it divides the array into a sorted section and an un-sorted section. Each pass adds at least one more item to the sorted section. Thus, at maximum, $n-1$ passes are needed to sort any array of length n (n passes are *not* needed since after $n-1$ items are arranged in order, the last item must also be in its proper place). The action of the algorithm indicates that the algorithm should stop when

a) the number of passes equals $n-1$ where n is the number of items in the array, or

b) no exchanges have been made in a pass (since that indicates that no items were out of order, i.e., that the array is all sorted).

When implemented, many algorithms actually do a "bubble-down" sorting, in which the "heaviest" (largest) item moves to the end the fastest.

The following is an example of the algorithm's operation:

Original array	25	57	48	37	12	92	86	33
check pair 1	(25	57)	48	37	12	92	86	33
no exchange needed								
check pair 2	25	(57	48)	37	12	92	86	33
exchange	25	(48	57)	37	12	92	86	33
check pair 3	25	48	(57	37)	12	92	86	33
exchange	25	48	(37	57)	12	92	66	33
check pair 4	25	48	37	(57	12)	92	86	33
exchange	25	48	37	(12	57)	92	86	33
check pair 5	25	48	37	12	(57	92)	86	33
no exchange needed								
check pair 6	25	48	37	12	57	(92	86)	33
exchange	25	48	37	12	57	(86	92)	33
check pair 7	25	48	37	12	57	86	(92	33)
exchange	25	48	37	12	57	86	(33	92)
after pass 1	25	48	37	12	57	86	33	**92**

Note that the greatest item is in its proper place at the last place in the array.

The same procedure of checking and exchanging (if necessary) is followed for each pass. The details are omitted. The results after the next two passes are:

after pass 2	25	37	12	48	57	33	**86**	**92**

Note that now the two largest items are in their proper places and order in the last two places in the array.

after pass 3   25   12   37   48   33   57   **86**   **92**

There are several ways to implement bubble sort. Note that after j passes, the last j elements are sorted and need never be looked at again. Thus most versions only check the first $n - j$ elements on pass $j + 1$. Also, the various versions differ as to which condition is used to determine when the algorithm should stop. The most inefficient method is to write the code so that all $n - 1$ passes are always performed (i.e., stopping condition (a)). A better way is to use a boolean variable (usually called a *flag*) to determine whether an exchange has taken place and stop if no exchanges have taken place in a particular pass (i.e., stopping condition (b)). Such a code is sometimes called a *flagged* bubble sort, and an example of it follows in Pascal.

PROCEDURE Bubblesort(VAR stuff:**ArrayType**; n:INTEGER);
(* This procedure sorts a 1-dimension array using the flagged bubble sort algorithm.
    The input array *stuff* is returned at the end of the procedure sorted with the minimum element in the first location and the maximum element in location n.
    The array is of type ArrayType and the number of elements in the array to be sorted is n. Each item in the array is a scalar variable of type ArrayItemType. *)

VAR exchanged : BOOLEAN;   (* the flag that indicates that an
                                  exchange has taken place *)
     pass,j   : INTEGER;   (* loop counters *)
     temp   : **ArrayItemType**; (* temporary variable for ex-
                                  changing elements in the array
                                  *)

```
BEGIN (* procedure bubblesort *)
        (* initialization *)
        exchanged := TRUE;
        pass := 0;
        (* checking and exchanging loop *)
        WHILE (pass < n – 1) AND exchanged DO
            BEGIN (* WHILE LOOP *)
                exchanged := FALSE;
                pass := pass + 1;
                FOR j := 1 TO n-pass DO
                (* check if adjacent items are out of order *)
                    If stuff[ j ] > stuff[ j+1] THEN
                        BEGIN (* exchange elements *)
                            temp := stuff[ j ];
                            stuff[ j ] := stuff[ j +1];
                            stuff[ j+1] := temp;
                            exchanged := TRUE
                        END (* IF and FOR *)
            END (* WHILE *)
END;    (* procedure bubblesort *)
```

The following code shows how the *bubblesort* procedure would be used.

```
PROGRAM Test (input,output);

TYPE   ArrayItemType = INTEGER;
       ArrayType = ARRAY[1...20] of ArrayItemType;

VAR    testarray : ArrayType;
       i : INTEGER;

BEGIN
        (* first initialize first 10 items in array *)
        FOR i:=1 TO 10 DO
```

```
            testarray[ i ] := 25 − i;
    (* bubblesort is now called, with a size parameter of 10,
        since only 10 items were given values and need be
        sorted *)
    bubblesort(testarray,10);
    (* the sorted array is now printed out *)
    FOR i:=1 TO 10 DO
        Writeln(testarray[ i ])
END.
```

In order to evaluate algorithms used with data structures, it is helpful to get some idea of how long they take to complete their task. A detailed analysis can be found elsewhere, but an overview is given here. Note that in pass *j*, the number of **comparisons** is *n − j*, and in the worst case, the number of passes is *n − 1*. Adding the number of comparisons together for each pass gives us *n(n − 1)/2 comparisons* in the **worst case**. Since the dominant term in this expression is a multiple of *n²*, this algorithm is said to be "of order n²" for the number of comparisons and this is written as $O(n^2)$. In the worst case, one **exchange** is performed for **each** comparison. Therefore, the number of exchanges equals *n(n − 1)/2 = O(n²)* for the **worst case**.

This formula is useful since it gives some indication of the speed of the algorithm relative to the size of the input. In particular, since $(2n)^2$ equals $4n^2$, if the size of the input is doubled, this indicates that it would take about four times longer to sort an array using bubble sort!

4.3   STRAIGHT SELECTION SORT

The most common example of a selection sort is the algorithm known as *straight selection* (or *jump down sort*).

The basic principle underlying this algorithm is this:

- — examine all the items in the **unsorted subsection** of the array and **select** the smallest [largest];
- — place the selected item in the first [last] place of the subsection being examined, reduce the size of the subsection.

As with the bubble sort, the algorithm consists of repeatingly performing *passes* on the array, each time applying the basic principle until the array is sorted. As with bubble sort, this algorithm also stops after $n - 1$ passes.

The following is an example of the algorithm's operation:

(array subscript)	1	2	3	4	5	6	7	8
original array	25	57	48	37	12	92	86	33

    subsection size = 8 — largest item is x[6] <=> 92
    x[6] is exchanged with x[8]

after pass 1	25	57	48	37	12	33	86	92

    subsection size = 7 — largest item is x[7] <=> 86
    x[7] is exchanged with x[7], i.e., nothing happens.

after pass 2	25	57	48	37	12	33	86	92

    subsection size = 6 — largest item is x[2] <=> 57
    x[2] is exchanged with x[6]

after pass 3	25	33	48	37	12	57	86	92

There are variations on the code for straight selection sort, but fewer than with bubble sort. There can be no "flagged" version of this sort, but there are fewer exchanges. The following is a version of it in Pascal.

```
PROCEDURE StraightSelection(VAR stuff:ArrayType;
                              n:INTEGER);
(*  This procedure sorts a 1-dimension array using the straight se-
    lection sort algorithm.
    The input array *stuff* is returned at the end of the procedure
    sorted with the minimum element in the first location and the
    maximum element in location n.
    The array is of type ArrayType and the number of elements in
    the array to be sorted is n. Each item in the array is a scalar
    variable of type ArrayItemType. *)


VAR  i,j,index    : INTEGER;
(*      i, j, and index are counters to be used as subscripts. *)
     large        : ArrayItemType
(*      large is the value of the largest element in *stuff* *)
BEGIN (* Procedure StraightSelection *)
        FOR i := n DOWNTO 2 DO
           BEGIN
           (* first initialize the "largest" item in *stuff* and save
              its subscript in index *)
               large := stuff[1];
               index := 1;
               (* check through the other elements to find
                  something "larger" *)
               FOR j := 2 TO i DO
                  IF stuff[ j ] > large THEN
               (* save the new large element and remember
                  its place *)
                     BEGIN
                        large := stuff[ j ];
                        index := j
                     END;  (* IF and FOR j *)
               (* completes the rest of the exchange *)
               stuff[index] := stuff[ i ];
```

```
                    stuff[ i ] := large
        END (* FOR i *)
END;    (* straightselection *)
```

In order to evaluate this algorithm, note that in pass j, the number of **comparisons** is $n - j$ and the number of passes is *always* $n - 1$. Adding the number of comparisons together for each pass again gives $n(n - 1)/2$ comparisons, written as $O(n^2)$. However, in this algorithm, there is only *one* exchange per pass. Thus, the total number of exchanges is $n - 1$ or $O(n)$.

Although this algorithm has significantly fewer exchanges than bubble sort, it still is slow because of the number of comparisons performed.

4.4   STABLE SORTS

Suppose an array of records with several fields is given, and suppose one field is called the *key* field. Let i and j be the indices of two records in this array and suppose *key[i] = key [j]*. In other words, suppose two records had the same ZIP code that is stored in the *key* field. Let us also suppose that, in the array, the ith record *precedes* the jth record. In other words, suppose the ith record corresponds to Mr. Brown's information and the jth record corresponds to Mrs. Smith's and the records are in alphabetical order.

A sort is called *stable* if, after sorting based on the *key* field, the record formerly associated with i still precedes the record formerly associated with j. In other words, a stable sort will not "undo" existing orders based on other keys, when sorting based on a different key and then examining items with equal key values.

The stability or non-stability of a sorting scheme can be an important consideration when several sorts are successively done on the same file. For example, suppose one wishes to alphabetize a list and then sort by ZIP code, hoping that the resulting list will show everyone who lives in the same ZIP code in alphabetical order. To ensure this, the second sort used *must* be stable.

Of the two elementary sorting schemes, bubble sort is *stable*, but straight selection sort is *not*. Thus, even though bubble sort makes more exchanges than straight selection sort, for certain applications it may actually be a preferred sorting scheme.

CHAPTER 5

SEARCHING

5.1   SEARCHING ALGORITHMS

It is often necessary to locate certain information stored in a data structure. To do this, consideration must be given to various possible ways of traversing the data structure in question. If a way can be found to traverse a data structure so that *every* cell can be accessed, then this method can also be used to search that structure for stored information. In this chapter, algorithms to search arrays will be examined. Traversals and searching algorithms for other data structures will also be considered in later chapters.

Frequently an array of records is searched according to one field to locate a specific record and be able to access and even modify other fields. Typical examples would include searching through a list of names to find (and retrieve) a telephone number, or searching a list of account numbers to modify a bank balance (or other related information).

The items actually searched are called *keys*. Usually a *key* is left unchanged, but another piece of information associated with the *key* is copied. Often this other piece of information is the index of the array element in which the desired item is stored. The index is then used to find what is really wanted, e.g., another field in the record of data. Frequently one field of a record is used as a key (e.g., the name field or the account number field), and other fields associated with the key (e.g., the telephone number or bank balance) are operated on (i.e., retrieved or modified).

There are two major search techniques associated with arrays: *Linear (Sequential) search* and *Binary search*.

Linear search can *always* be used. The underlying principle is to examine each element of an array in order, starting at the first one, until the desired *key* is found. This method is particularly suited for an *unsorted* array, and can be considered similar to the procedure often used for searching a shuffled deck of cards for a given card.

Binary search can be used *only* with a *sorted* array. It is a stylized version of what someone does when searching a telephone book for a number. In general, one starts in the *middle*, and keeps eliminating part of the book until the desired name is found. (Note again for the sake of emphasis, that when the name is found in the book, it is not copied since it is already known, but rather, the *associated information* of the *phone number* is copied and used.)

5.2 LINEAR SEARCH

Linear search (sometimes called *sequential search*) is a straightforward algorithm that starts with examining the first key in the array and continues until it finds the desired item or it reaches the end of the array (without finding it). When the algorithm finds the item, it returns the array index of the item in the parameter *place*. If the desired item is *not* found, the final value of *place* is zero. If two or more records in the array have the same key, only the first one is located. This algorithm can be used with either sorted or unsorted arrays. The following is a version of the algorithm in Pascal.

```pascal
PROCEDURE LinSearch (stuff:ArrayType; n:INTEGER;
                     key:ArrayItemType; VAR place: INTEGER);

(*  STUFF is the array of records being searched,
    N is the number of items being searched
    (which may be less than the total size if the array is not full)
KEY is the key item being searched for,
    PLACE indicates where KEY is in the array, or if it is zero,
    indicates that KEY was NOT FOUND *)

VAR    i      : INTEGER;
       found  : BOOLEAN;

BEGIN
        (* initialization *)
        found := FALSE;
        i := 1;  (* the first item in the array is assumed to have
                    subscript 1 *)
        place := 0;
        (* search loop *)
        WHILE (i <= n) AND (NOT found) DO
            IF key = stuff[ i ] THEN (* we have found it! *)
                BEGIN place := i; (* location of KEY in stuff *)
        found := TRUE (* flag to get out of loop *)
                END
            ELSE
                i := i + 1;
END; (* procedure *)
```

The following segment gives an example of how to use this code in a program.

```
(* assume that AccountNumbers contains Num account
   numbers *)
Read(key);
linsearch(AccountNumbers,Num,key,location);
write('Account',key', is stored in location',location);
```

A brief analysis of the efficiency of linear search is appropriate. In the worst case, the sought-after item is not in the array, but every element in the array will have been examined in the attempt to find it. If there are *n* items, then the number of comparisons is *n*. Therefore, for the number of comparisons, linear search is $O(n)$ in the worst case.

5.3 BINARY SEARCH

To understand how **binary search** works, its operation is demonstrated by the following example.

The location of account number 350 in the following array of account numbers is sought.

subscript	1	2	3	4	5	6	7	8
CONTENTS	110	112	156	210	257	296	350	892
	^1			^1				^1
	F			M				L

(The digits "1" above the letters F, M, and L indicate the *first* values of these variables that point to elements in the array.) Initially, the entire array is examined. Thus *F*irst initially points to the item 1 and *L*ast points to item 8. The "*M*iddle" item is computed by the formula:

$$M = (F + L) \text{ div } 2.$$

The **div** operator gives an integer result, e.g., 5 div 2 is 2 and not 2.50.)

With F being 1 and L being 8, M is 4, as shown above.

Next, what is sought (i.e., 350) is compared to what is in the 4th element of the array (i.e., 210). Since what is sought (350) is greater than the "middle" item, the middle element and the first half of the list are ignored. This "ignoring" of the first half is accomplished by resetting F to be one past the middle item, i.e., $F = M + 1$. F is now 5, and the procedure is started again (and the fact that there ever was a first half of the array is ignored). Thus the following situation now exists:

subscript	1	2	3	4	5	6	7	8
CONTENTS	110	112	156	210	257	296	350	892
					^2	^2		^2
					F	M		L

$F + L = 5 + 8 = 13$
$\Rightarrow M = 13$ div $2 = 6$

Since $M = 6$ is not the correct array location, F is recomputed: $F = M + 1 = 6 + 1 = 7$, resulting in:

subscript	1	2	3	4	5	6	7	8
CONTENTS	110	112	156	210	257	296	350	892
							^3	^3
							F	L
							^3	
							M	

$F + L = 7 + 8 = 15$
$\Rightarrow M = 15$ div $2 = 7$
ARRAY[middle] = ARRAY[7] = 350 which is what was sought!

The code of the algorithm which follows merely translates this procedure.

```
PROCEDURE BinSearch (Stuff:ArrayType; n:INTEGER;
                       key:ArrayItemType; VAR place: INTEGER;

(* parameters have the same purpose as in linear search *)

VAR first, last, middle : INTEGER;

BEGIN
        (* initialization *)
        first := 1;
        last := n;
        place := 0;
        (* major loop *)
        WHILE first <= last DO
            BEGIN
                middle := (first + last) DIV 2;
                IF key = stuff[middle] THEN
                (* we have found it! *)
                    BEGIN
                        first := last + 1;
                        (* trick to get out of loop *)
                        place := middle
                        (* save location of KEY *)
                    END
                ELSE (* we have not found it but which half
                    do we ignore ? *)
                    IF key > stuff[middle] THEN
                    (* omit first half *)
                        first := middle + 1
                    ELSE (* omit last half *)
                        last := middle - 1
            END (* while *)
END; (* procedure *)
```

A brief analysis of the efficiency of binary search is also appropriate. The worst case is related to how many times the array size can be subdivided in half and still be an integer. The calculations are easier if the size of the array, n, is assumed to be a power of 2, e.g., $n = 2^i$ for some i. A careful analysis shows that in this case, the maximum number of times that the array can be divided by 2 is i.

But $\log_2 n = \log_2(2^i) = i$.

Therefore, at worst, there are $i = \log_2 n$ subdivisions and, for each subdivision there are at most *two* comparisons in the loop of the code given above. In other words, in the worst case, the number of comparisons is $O(\log_2 n)$.

To compare linear search with binary search, if $n = 1024$, the *linear* search worst case = *1024 comparisons*, and the *binary* search worst case = $2 \times \log_2 1024 = 2 \times \log_2 2^{10} = $ *20 comparisons*.

5.4 HASHING

5.4.1 PRELIMINARIES

There are situations that arise in which information needs to be retrieved from a data structure quickly, but even the use of binary search with arrays is too slow. Binary search would also be difficult to use if the array were constantly being updated by insertions and deletions, since using binary search would demand that an array be adjusted so it remains sorted after each insertion or deletion, a process that could slow down the procedure even more. (Linear search would be even slower, although there would be no need to sort after insertions.) An alternative is to dispense with any ordering and instead use a *hash function*.

A **hash function**, h, is a function that maps a *key* (i.e., one field in a record) into an *address* (i.e., array subscript) that is then used to store the associated record (in that array). If the symbol S designates some key (e.g., a number or character), then $h(S)$ is its hash address or hash number. *Hashing* refers to the use of hash functions for data storage and retrieval.

For a specific set of keys, an ideal hash function is bijective (i.e., $1 - 1$, unique). In other words, the ideal function is one that makes two different keys correspond to two different addresses, yet is easy to compute. However, such a function is rarely, if ever, obtained.

When two symbols S_1 and S_2 are used as keys and when $h(S_1)$ equals $h(S_2)$ for the hash function h, then a **hash collision** or **hash clash** is said to have occurred. Good hash functions are those that lead to few such collisions, but since collisions regularly occur, procedures exist to resolve the resulting difficulties.

The *general procedure for using a hash function* to store and retrieve information is as follows:

(1)   Given the key symbol **S**, compute its hash value, **h(S)**;

(2)   Access the record in the data storage structure (normally an array) corresponding to **h(S)**;

(3)   If a collision occurs, resolve any ambiguities.

5.4.2   HASH FUNCTIONS

There are different possibilities for hash functions, and no one function is ideal for all purposes. The major types of functions are now briefly mentioned.

5.4.2.1 DIVISION

This is the earliest type of hash functions. It is very widely used and is one of the easiest functions to calculate. It presupposes a range in which the output of the function lies, e.g., the permitted values for the array subscript. If the elements are to be stored in an array of size m, the hash function would be

$$h(x) = x \bmod m \text{ (if the range were 0 to } m - 1\text{)}$$
$$\text{or}$$
$$h(x) = (x \bmod m) + 1 \text{ (if the range were 1 to } m\text{)}.$$

The modulus m is usually chosen to be a prime number slightly larger than the number of elements to be stored. As an example, with $m = 11$, $h(35) = (35 \bmod 11) + 1 = 2 + 1 = 3$. It has been suggested that a prime of the form $4k + 3$ for some integer k is particularly effective as a modulus.

The major problem with this type of hash function is that it is very easy to get clashes. For example, if m is 101,

$$h(125) = 125 \bmod 101 + 1 = 24 + 1 = 25.$$
$$h(226) = 226 \bmod 101 + 1 = 24 + 1 = 25.$$

5.4.2.2 MIDSQUARE

This method attempts to introduce a certain randomness into the computation of the hash number, and can be viewed as a specific version of a more general approach of computing a hash number by means of a (repeatable) *random number generator*. In other words, given two different keys, the hash function should produce two different numbers with little or no relationship to the keys or to each other, except that the same function will produce the same hash numbers given the same input anytime it is used.

41

The name "mid-square" is derived from the steps taken by the hash function to produce a result: taking the *mid*dle of the *square* of the input number. In other words, given x, one first squares it, and then removes the center few digits to use as the hash number. This method is sometimes used as a random number generator. It can be formulated as:

$$h(x) = (x^2 \text{ div } n) \text{ mod } n$$

where $n = 10^i$ or 2^i for some i. For example, if x equals 123456

then	x^2 =	1524**138**3936.
If	n =	10^4,
then	$h(x)$ =	138.

5.4.2.3 FOLDING

This method is sometimes called *bit* or *digit compression*. The general strategy is: (1) *subdivide* the key x into groups of n-digits (bits) (the leading or last group can have fewer than n-digits or bits); (2) *combine* the different groups together by an operation such as *sum, exclusive-or*, or *or*; (3) *extract* the last n digits (bits) of the resulting number as the hash number (i.e., mod the number by 10^n if it has more than n digits). For example, with n being 3,

$$h(97434658) = (974+346+58) \text{ mod } 1000$$
$$= 1378 \text{ mod } 1000 = \mathbf{378}$$
$$h(31269857) = (312+698+57) \text{ mod } 1000$$
$$= 1067 \text{ mod } 1000 = \mathbf{67}$$

5.4.2.4 DIGIT ANALYSIS

This is sometimes called *digit* or *character* or *bit extraction*. The general strategy is: (1) *select* certain digits (bits) of the key *x*; (2) **transform or re-arrange** them as the hash number. The following procedure may be taken as a simple example of this approach:

(1)   Take the digits in positions 3 – 6,

and   (2)   Reverse them.

Thus, $h(75{:}4612{:}3) = 2164$

This approach is less desirable than others since, in general, it is better to use a method that makes use of **all** the input information, i.e., all bits or digits. However, in some situations, some of the input information is biased and can skew the computation of a hash number. For example, the majority of social security numbers begin with either the digit 5 or the digit 3. It would be better to ignore the first digit and use the other digits, perhaps transforming them by one of the other types of hash functions.

5.4.2.5 MULTIPLICATION

This method derives its name from the two multiplications involved in obtaining the hash number. The combination of multiplication and other arithmetic operations suggests that the resulting hash numbers will be more evenly distributed throughout the storage array. It can be formulated as:

$$h(x) = \text{trunc}(m * \text{fraction}(x * z))$$

where *m* is the size of the storage array, *z* is a number between 0 and 1, **trunc** is the truncation function (that eliminates the fractional part of a number) and **fraction** eliminates the integral part of a number. The resulting number will be an integer between 0 and *m* and could possibly be 0. Some studies indicate that the best choice of *z* is $(\sqrt{5}-1)/2$ or $1 - (\sqrt{5}-1)/2$.

EXAMPLE

Suppose the following records are to be stored via a hashing scheme:

ID # (key)	Name	Other Information
2651	Smith	...
3412	Jones	...
1183	Brown	...
9356	Kelly	...

(1) Using **Digit Analysis**, by taking digits 2 and 4 and adding them, the following hash numbers are obtained:

ID # (key)	Hash Numbers
2651	$6 + 1 = 7$
3412	$4 + 2 = 6$
1183	$1 + 3 = 4$
9356	$3 + 6 = 9$

Therefore, the storage array would look like:

1	2	3	4	5	6	7	8	9	10
			1183 Brown		3511 Jones	2651 Smith		9356 Kelly	

(2) Using a **Division** method, with $m = 10$ (including the shift by 1), the following are obtained:

ID # (key)	Hash Numbers
2651	2
3412	3
1183	4
9356	7

44

Therefore, the storage array would look like:

1	2	3	4	5	6	7	8	9	10
	2651 Smith	3412 Jones	1183 Brown			9356 Kelly			

CHAPTER 6

LINKED LISTS

6.1 BASIC DEFINITIONS

6.1.1 LISTS AND NODES

A **linked list** is an ADT (abstract data type) consisting of a collection of items called **nodes**. Each node is a record containing at least two fields, an *information* field (usually abbreviated to *info*) and a *next address* field (sometimes called a *link* field). The simplest type of linked list has only one address field and is called a *singly linked list*. However, there may be multiple information fields in each node. The *address field* contains the address of the next node on the list, i.e., the memory location that begins the next node.

The *address* of a node is frequently called a **pointer** to a node.

The **first node** in a list (to which no other node points) is called the **head** of the list. The **last node** in a list (which does not point to any other node) is called the **tail**.

The "dummy" address that points nowhere is called the **nil pointer** or **null pointer** or simply **nil** (or **null**). It is used as an address in the *next* field of a tail node to indicate the end of a list and is often depicted with a slash bar (/) through the *next* field of a node.

A list with no nodes is called the **empty list** or the **nil list**.

6.1.2 POINTERS

As mentioned above, a pointer is merely an *address* to a node, i.e., to a memory location. The pointer variable that points to the head node is commonly also used to designate the entire list.

Specific programming languages have various ways to implement linked lists. Many languages (such as Pascal, C, Ada, Modula-2) include pointer variables, and these are commonly used to implement linked lists as will be explained below. Because Pascal is so widely used, many authors use the Pascal pointer notation when referring to linked lists, though other notations exist to reference nodes of linked lists and their components. Pascal uses an uparrow (caret) after a pointer variable to indicate the "node to which a pointer points." For example, if *p* is a pointer variable, then *p*^ is the "node to which the pointer variable *p* points."

The distinction between a pointer (pointer variable) and the item pointed to can be confusing, and this confusion can be a source of programming errors. It is necessary to be clear about the distinction. Thus, the following example, taken from a non-computer environment, may help clarify the difference.

Suppose a town has a hospital named Mercy whose address is 1400 West Park. Suppose several blocks away (at Sixth and White Streets) there is a sign that points to Mercy Hospital and suppose someone named the sign "Sam." Sam is not Mercy Hospital. Sam is merely a street sign, but Sam points to Mercy Hospital. To use Pascal notation, Sam is a street sign at Sixth and White, the value of Sam is 1400 West Park, and Sam^ is Mercy Hospital. The address of Mercy Hospital (1400 West Park) is different than the address of Sam (Sixth and White). The two are interrelated yet distinctively different. In a similar way, *p* is not a node, but merely points to (gives the address of) a node. *p* and *p*^ are located in two different places in computer memory, but are interrelated.

6.1.3 DIAGRAMMING LISTS AND EXAMPLES

The ADT of a linked list is normally depicted by using divided *boxes* to indicate *nodes* and *arrows* to indicate *pointers* to nodes as in the following diagram:

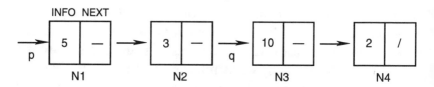

This list has four nodes that can be labeled *N1, N2, N3,* and *N4.* (In most programs, such labels of individual nodes in a linked list are never used.) The *head node* is *N1* and the *tail node* is *N4.* Node *N4* has a nil pointer depicted in its *next* section. *p* is the name of the pointer to node *N1,* but since *N1* is the head node, *p* is also considered the pointer to the entire list.

The pointer between node *N2* and node *N3* is also labeled *q* for purposes of example. Using Pascal notation, node *N1* usually designated as *p*^ and node *N3* as *q*^. Thus, *p*^.*info* is 5 and *p*^.*next* is a pointer variable pointing to the node *N2*. So, *p*^.*next*^.*info* is 3. Similarly, *q*^.*next*^.*info* is 2 and *q*^.*next*^.*next* is NIL.

A second related diagram may help clarify the difference between pointers and nodes pointed to. Nodes are combinations of two or more memory locations, one used to store information, one used to store the address of the next node. These two memory locations can be assumed to be adjacent. As was emphasized earlier, in memory a computer stores only numbers — it cannot store the arrows used in diagrams. The following diagram emphasizes this by using numbers in place of arrows.

	Memory Location	Contents	Node Name	
(p-pointer)	2501	2813		Mem. loc. 2814 is a
(q-pointer)	2502	4559		pointer to the next
	...			node that consists
	2813	5	N1	of the 2 mem. loc.'s
	2814	2815		2815 & 2816.
	2815	3	N2	
	2816	4559		
	...			
	3218	2	N4	
	3219	0<nil>		
	...			
	4559	10	N3	— info field
	4560	3218		— next field

The numbers contained in the *next* fields of the nodes depicted in this second diagram did not appear in the original diagram since the arrows took their places. The numbers have replaced the arrows since arrows cannot exist in computer memory. Even though the two diagrams are significantly different, they nevertheless contain the *same* information. Note also that the second diagram emphasizes the difference between a pointer variable and what it points to. *p* is at memory location 2501, but *p* points to memory location 2813 which is where node *N1* is located.

6.1.4 LISTS AND ARRAYS

Lists have several advantages over arrays in certain situations. A major advantage is the *dynamic allocation* of nodes in a list as opposed to the unchanging *static* allocation of arrays. In other words, a program can request more space for lists when needed at *run time*, rather than pre-determining all the space at *compile time* as with arrays.

Another advantage involves inserting items into and removing items from the data structure. It is difficult to insert a new item into a sorted array in the correct location. Many items need to be shifted and there may be no room for more information. Similarly, deleting an item from an array means that many other items must be moved to fill in the gap. Such operations are relatively trivial with linked lists since only one or two pointers need to be shifted and none of the other items in the list need to be shifted. For example, suppose an item needs to be added to a list in a specific place, say right after node $p^\wedge$. First a new node, say $q^\wedge$, is created, then $q^\wedge.next$ is set to point to $p^\wedge.next$, and the $p^\wedge.next$ is reset to q. (See the diagram in section 6.4.2.) None of the other elements in the list needs to be shifted.

There can be disadvantages associated with lists as well. A list is a **sequential access structure** (rather than a random access structure as with an array). To access any item in a list, one must start at the head of the list and move through the list, one node at a time, until the desired node is reached. Another disadvantage concerns computer memory. For each node, not only is room to store the information needed, but also an extra memory location to store the address of the next node. This illustrates the trade off that occurs many times in computer science: to gain some advantages, one endures a loss of some available memory.

Up to this point, linked lists have been discussed as ADTs without referring to implementation. The various operations on lists could also be described in detail solely by using box and arrow diagrams. Actual implementation techniques will be discussed next. As mentioned in Chapter 1, implementation of ADTs should be done in such a way that the implementation can be changed or improved without significant change to the program that uses the ADT.

6.1.5 IMPLEMENTING LISTS

There are two major ways of implementing a linked list:

1) *explicitly* using an *array* of available list nodes (called the *linear* implementation of linked lists);

2) *implicitly* using the special features of a given language, such as pointer variables and records (called the *pointer* implementation of linked lists). Languages that have pointer variables as a built-in data type hide most of the messy bookkeeping necessary to keep the pointers straight.

6.2 LINEAR IMPLEMENTATION

6.2.1 UNDERLYING DATA STRUCTURE

The ADT of a linked list can be implemented by using an array of records, such that each array element is a node. This implementation may be necessary if the language being used does not have pointer variables.

Initially an array of nodes is explicitly declared and made large enough so that the program would never run out of nodes for linked lists. For example (using Pascal),

```
CONST   numbernodes = 500;

TYPE   nodetype   = RECORD
                        info : INTEGER;
```

51

```
                    next : INTEGER;
                END;

VAR     nodesupply  :  ARRAY[1. .numbernodes] OF nodetype;
```

6.2.2 PRESUPPOSITIONS

Certain presuppositions regarding our data structure and how it will be used need to be determined.

The array *nodesupply* will be used as the supply of all available nodes and nodes will be "obtained from it" as well as "returned to it" when no longer needed. In reality, the nodes themselves always remain in the array, and "active" nodes (that are part of one or more active linked lists) may be intermingled with "inactive" nodes (that are available for use). The inactive nodes and the various lists of active nodes are kept separate by the way they are linked together through the *next* fields.

The "pointer" that will be stored in the *next* field of each node will be the *index* of the array *nodesupply* where the next node is located.

To simplify the code, the array of nodes, *nodesupply*, the total number of nodes, *numbernodes*, and the pointer to the next available node, *avail*, are assumed to be global variables.

6.2.3 INITIALIZATION

The array *nodesupply* needs to be initialized so that the next available node can always be found. This is done by setting the pointers so that *nodesupply[i]* links to *nodesupply[i + 1]* resulting in a linked list of available nodes that will be referred to as the "available list." Without this initialization and linkage, there would be no easy way to distinguish which nodes are available and which are part of active lists. The initialization is done via the following procedure.

```
PROCEDURE Initialize;
VAR i: INTEGER;
BEGIN
        (* Link first numbernodes−1 nodes to successors *)
        FOR i:= 1 TO numbernodes−1 DO
            nodesupply[ i ].next := i + 1;
        (* Link last node to nil-pointer = 0 *)
        nodesupply[numbernodes].next := 0;
        avail := 1
END;    (* Initialize *)
```

This code makes *nodesupply[i]* point to *nodesupply[i + 1]* and the last node point to 0, which is the signal for a *nil* pointer. It ends by setting *avail* equal to 1, indicating that the first element in the *nodesupply* array is the first available node for use by a list.

6.2.4   OBTAINING AND RELEASING NODES

When a node is needed, it is taken from the head of the available list. When a node from an active list is disposed of, it is tacked onto the head of this available list. Thus, it may be that at some point of a running program, the head of the available list may be *nodesupply[23]* which links to *nodesupply[12]* which links to *nodesupply[50]* which links to *nodesupply[51]*, etc. This fact helps explain the code of the next section.

6.2.5   OBTAINING A NODE FROM THE AVAILABLE LIST

The following procedure takes a node from the available list for use by a list. The available list is properly altered.

```
PROCEDURE Getnode(VAR p: INTEGER);
BEGIN
```

```
        IF avail = 0 THEN
            Writeln('list overflow') (* error *)
        ELSE
            BEGIN
                p := avail;
                avail := nodesupply[avail].next
            END
END;    (* Getnode *)
```

The initialization procedure set *nodesupply[i].next* equal
to *i + 1*. But note that *avail* is *not* merely incremented by 1,
since, as mentioned above, after getting nodes for lists and
freeing nodes, it may be that the original "natural" link order is
totally re-arranged. Instead, it has been set to what the *next*
field says the next available node is.

6.2.6 RETURNING (FREEING) A NODE TO THE AVAILABLE LIST

A program may need so many nodes that all the nodes
created in the *nodesupply* array may be used up. However, not
all nodes may be actively part of any list at any one moment of
the program. By somehow returning inactive nodes to the
available list, an "overflow" (i.e., running out of available
nodes) can be avoided. This is the purpose of the following
procedure. In addition, if one does not de-allocate (i.e., free up)
the node space at an appropriate point of a program, one may
lose a pointer to the node and *not* be able to use it or dispose of
it later.

When a node is freed up and returned to the available list, it
is placed at the *head*. The *next* section of this freed node is set
to point to the old head of the available list, and the pointer to
the first available node (*avail*) is adjusted to point to this last
node freed.

54

```
PROCEDURE ReturnNode (p: INTEGER);
BEGIN
        nodesupply[p].next := avail;
        avail := p
END;    (* ReturnNode *)
```

EXAMPLES

Example A — Creating a List.

To create an ADT of a linked list (regardless of how it is implemented) the following steps are needed:

(1)   create a new node;
(2)   give a value to the **info** section of the node;
(3)   link up the **next** section to another node.

The following code recursively generates a list of length *n* by getting a node and then generating a list of length *n − 1* which it points to. The information section of each node is filled with the number of its reverse order in the list, i.e., the head node contains *n*, etc. Code such as this is purely for demonstration purposes and would never be used in a major program.

```
FUNCTION Genlist(n : INTEGER) : INTEGER;
        (* Recursive code *)
VAR    p: INTEGER;
BEGIN
        Getnode(p);
        If n>1 THEN
            nodesupply[p].next := Genlist(n–1)
        ELSE
            nodesupply[p].next := 0;
        nodesupply[p].info := n;
        Genlist := p
END;    (* Genlist *)
```

Example B — Printing a List

```
PROCEDURE Printlist(list: INTEGER);
        (* Iterative code *)
BEGIN
        WHILE list <> 0 DO
            BEGIN
                Writeln(nodesupply[list].info);
                list := nodesupply[list].next
            END (* WHILE *)
END;    (* Printlist *)
```

6.3 POINTER IMPLEMENTATION

6.3.1 DEFINING POINTER TYPES AND DECLARING POINTER VARIABLES

To implement the ADT of a linked list using pointer variables in those languages that possess them (e.g., C, Pascal, Modula-2, Ada), normally *two* new types are defined: one is a pointer variable type, the other a node type. In Pascal, for example, one could write:

```
Type ptr  =  ^node;
     node =  RECORD
                info: INTEGER;
                next:ptr
             END;
```

(Note that in Pascal, in the TYPE definition, the uparrow [or caret] comes *before* the type identifier of what it points to. This is the only case in Pascal where an identifier [e.g., "node"] can be used without being first declared.)

After the definition of the new types, variables of the type **ptr** are merely declared. For example,

56

```
VAR p,q,list : ptr;
```

Note that the pointer variables *p*, *q*, and *list* exist, but they are places to keep addresses only. As yet, *no nodes have been created*!

6.3.2 OBTAINING NODES — THE PASCAL *NEW* PROCEDURE

In Pascal, nodes are created using the standard Pascal procedure **New** that takes a **pointer** variable as an argument. For example, the following code segment takes a declared pointer variable *p*, and then allocates space for a node of the type that *p* points to. After this "new" space has been allocated, the fields of the node are given values.

```
New(p);
p^.info := 5
p^.next := NIL;
```

New allows a programmer to *dynamically* create as *many* nodes as needed, *when* they are needed. *New* does for pointer variables what *Getnode* in Section 6.2.5 did for the linear implementation.

6.3.3 RELEASING NODES — THE PASCAL *DISPOSE* PROCEDURE

Pascal allows a programmer to dispose of unneeded nodes by using the library procedure *Dispose*, which also takes a pointer variable as an argument. The node pointed to then becomes part of the available space for use. Thus *dispose* functions like the procedure ReturnNode in Section 6.2.6 above. In a Pascal program, one simply writes

```
Dispose(p);
```

57

After this procedure call, *p* no longer points to any valid node, and if one tries to use *p^* (without first obtaining a node by using *New(p))*, one normally gets an error.

EXAMPLES
Example A — Creating a List
Much of the code that follows is **very** similar to the code presented in Section 6.2.7 that used the linear (array) implementation of lists. The logic underlying each of the functions is unchanged — only the actual implementation of the ADT of a linked list has changed, and thus, the only changes in the code of the various procedures and functions are those that are necessary for the new implementation.

```
FUNCTION Genlist(n : INTEGER) : ptr;
        (* Recursive code *)
VAR     p: ptr;
BEGIN
        New(p);
        If n > 1 THEN
            p^.next := Genlist(n–1)
        ELSE
            p^.next := NIL;
        p^.info := n;
        Genlist := p
END;    (* Genlist *)
```

Example B — Printing a List

```
PROCEDURE Printlist(list:ptr);
        (* Iterative code *)
BEGIN
        WHILE list <> NIL DO
            BEGIN
                Writeln(list^.info);
                list := list^.next
```

```
        END (* WHILE *)
END;   (* Printlist *)
```

6.4   COMMON OPERATIONS

6.4.1   TYPES OF OPERATIONS

Operations for the ADT of a linked list can be determined without knowing anything about a particular implementation. For example, some or all of the following might be desired:

```
PROCEDURE Create(Var list:ptr);
        (to create a new list with one node)
FUNCTION IsListEmpty(list:ptr):BOOLEAN;
        (to test to see if the list is empty)
PROCEDURE InsAfter(p:ptr; x:item);
        (to insert x after the node that p points to)
PROCEDURE InsEnd(list:ptr; x:item);
        (to insert x at the end of the list that list points to)
PROCEDURE DelAfter(p:ptr);
        (to delete the node after the node that p points to)
FUNCTION Search(list:ptr; x:item):ptr;
        (to search a list for an item and return a pointer to the correct
          node)
```

Not all of the operations listed above will be shown below. Enough samples are given to enable other routines to be written.

For now, it is presupposed that the "position pointer" p used as a parameter actually points to the node one suspects it points to. There are other alternatives possible, and one will be mentioned below in Section 6.5.1. Choosing different presuppositions or variations on the basic linked list structure (see Section 6.5 below) may lead to a different set of basic operations or an easier implementation of those chosen.

59

6.4.2 INSERTION

First, a consideration of what any insertion routine must do for a list as an ADT is presented before any code for specific implementations of lists is seen. A new node needs to be inserted after the node to which *p* points, and then information *x* is placed into the *info* section of that node. To do this, first a new node is obtained, then its *next* pointer is assigned to the node to which *p^.next* points, and then *p^.next* is re-assigned to point to the new node. This process can be envisioned by using a diagram of the ADT of a linked list as follows.

Notice that existing information in the list is *not* re-arranged. This property of linked lists makes them a preferred data structure when many insertions (and/or deletions) take place.

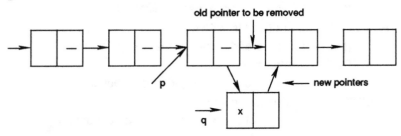

The following two sections of code present the procedure *InsAfter* (for "Insert After") based on the two different implementations discussed above.

A. ARRAY IMPLEMENTATION

```
PROCEDURE InsAfter (p:INTEGER;x:INTEGER);
VAR    q:INTEGER;
BEGIN
        IF p = 0 THEN (* check to see if p is nil *)
            Writeln('Void insertion') (* error *)
        ELSE
```

```
        BEGIN
            Getnode(q);
            nodesupply[q].info := x;
            nodesupply[q].next := nodesupply[p].next;
            nodesupply[p].next := q
        END (* IF..ELSE *)
END;   (* InsAfter *)
```

B. POINTER IMPLEMENTATION

```
PROCEDURE InsAfter (p:ptr; x:item);
VAR    q:ptr;
BEGIN
        IF p = NIL THEN (* check to see if p is nil *)
            Writeln('Void insertion') (* error *)
        ELSE
            BEGIN
                New(q);
                q^.info := x;
                q^.next := p^.next;
                p^.next := q
            END (* IF..ELSE *)
END;   (* InsAfter *)
```

Sometimes a special procedure is desirable for tacking on new nodes to the *end* of existing lists. The following procedure ***InsEnd*** (for "Insert at End") performs that task, given the pointer to the *list* (rather than to a *node* as in the previous code). The procedure first creates the new tail node, and then uses the pointer *q* to locate the old tail node and then connects it to the new node.

```
PROCEDURE InsEnd (VAR list:ptr; x:item);
VAR    p,q:ptr;
BEGIN
```

```
(* create and fill new node *)
New(p);
p^.info := x;
p^.next := NIL;
IF list = NIL THEN
    list := p
ELSE (* search for end of the list *)
    BEGIN
        q := list;
        WHILE q^.next <> NIL DO
            q:=q^.next;
            (* reset former nil-pointer to point to the
              new node *)
        q^.next := p
    END (* IF..ELSE *)
END;   (* InsEnd *)
```

6.4.3 DELETION

First, a consideration of what any deletion routine must do for a list as an ADT is presented before code for specific implementations of lists is seen. A procedure "DelAfter" that deletes the node *after* the node pointed to by *p* and returns the value of its *info* section in the variable *x* is to be created. It must check whether the proposed deletion is valid by checking to see if the list has more than one node. It deletes a node by re-directing the pointer of the previous node to point to the following node. This process can again be envisioned by using a diagram of the ADT of a linked list as follows.

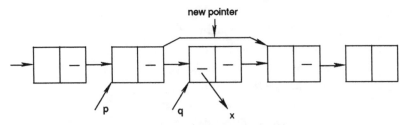

new pointer

p   q   x

The following two sections of code present the procedure
DelAfter based on the two different implementations discussed
above.

A. ARRAY IMPLEMENTATION

```
PROCEDURE DelAfter (p:INTEGER; VAR x:INTEGER);
VAR    q:INTEGER;
BEGIN
        IF p = 0 THEN (* nil pointer *)
            Writeln('Void deletion')
        ELSE
            IF nodesupply[p].next = 0 THEN
                (* no next node *)
                    Writeln('Void deletion')
            ELSE
                BEGIN
                    q:nodesupply[p].next;
                    x:nodesupply[q].info;
                    nodesupply[p].next=nodesupply[q].next;
                    ReturnNode(q)
                END (* else *)
END;    (* DelAfter *)
```

B. POINTER IMPLEMENTATION

```
PROCEDURE DelAfter (p:ptr; VAR x:item);
VAR    q:ptr;
```

```
BEGIN
        IF p = NIL THEN (* nil pointer *)
            Writeln('Void deletion')
        ELSE
            IF p^.next = NIL THEN
                (* no next node *)
                    Writeln('Void deletion')
            ELSE
                BEGIN
                    q := p^.next;
                    x := q^.info;
                    p^.next:=q^.next;
                    Dispose(q)
                END (* IF..ELSE IF..ELSE *)
END;    (* DelAfter *)
```

6.4.4   SEARCHING

This next function is basically a "linear search" scheme for linked lists (rather than arrays). The list *list* is searched for *x* and the function *Search* returns the pointer to the *first* node containing *x*.

```
FUNCTION Search(list:ptr; x:item):ptr;
VAR    p:ptr;
       found:boolean;
BEGIN
        p := list;
        found := FALSE;
        WHILE (p <> NIL) AND (NOT found) DO
            IF p^.info = x THEN
                found := TRUE
            ELSE
                p := p^.next;
        Search := p
END;    (* Search *)
```

This *Search* function may not be useful in certain situations, as when the node containing *x* needs to be deleted. In this case, the pointer to the *previous* node is needed rather than to the node containing *x*. *Search* can be easily modified to return two pointers, and the interior code expanded to retain the previous value of *p*.

The efficiency of this search is the same as for the linear search for arrays, i.e., it is *O(n)* for a list of *n* nodes. Since lists are sequential access structures (as mentioned above in Section 6.1.4), it is impossible to develop a routine for lists comparable to binary search for arrays with the same efficiency.

6.5 VARIATIONS

6.5.1 HEADER NODES

It is occasionally desirable to keep some bookkeeping information about a list, e.g., the number of nodes in the list, the use of the list, etc. Depending on the conventions decided upon when coding a procedure or function, it may even be desirable to have a "dummy" node in which no information is stored.

To store the bookkeeping information, one can use another node, called the *header node*, which itself points to the first (active and regular) node of the list. In this arrangement, even the "empty" list has one node, its header node.

The use of a header node means that most of the list routines need minor modifications. However, with a header node, certain applications may be simplified.

For example, if a "dummy" header node is used, the notion of a position pointer to a node (i.e., the pointer used as a parameter in routines) could be re-defined. The *coded* pointer could be implemented as the *actual* pointer to the *previous* node. Using this implementation, for a delete routine, only the "pointer" to the node to be deleted is needed (since it is actually the pointer to the previous node) (see discussion above in Section 6.4.1 and 6.4.4).

This brief example again shows some of the trade-offs involved in working with data structures and related algorithms. We sometimes choose to make a data structure slightly more complicated (e.g., by including a header node) and to modify our meaning of a "pointer to a node." One result is that the code for our routines will need to be developed with more care (to avoid any errors due to the new meaning of "pointer"). However, the end result is a set of routines that will be easier to use in programs that need them.

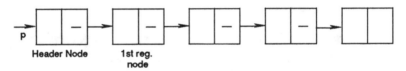

P

Header Node   1st reg.
               node

6.5.2 CIRCULAR LISTS

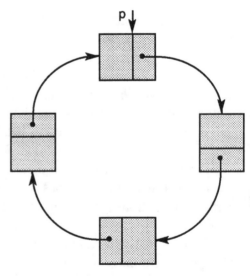

It is often convenient to have the *next* field of the end node of a list *not* be *NIL*, but rather point back to the head of the list. This convention makes the list *circular*.

In some situations, a circular list can be a better data structure than a non-circular list. For example, it is always possible to reach any node from any other node since by going forward, eventually one reaches the head of the list. Examples of the use of circular lists will be seen in subsequent chapters when various implementations of ADTs are discussed.

6.5.3 DOUBLY LINKED LISTS

A major problem with linked lists is the *in*-ability to back up. This problem can be eliminated by using both a *forward* (right link) and also a *backward* (left link) pointer, which results in a new ADT of a "Doubly-Linked List." It is also impossible with regular linked lists to delete a node of a linked list, given just the actual pointer to the node (unless the technique mentioned in Section 6.5.1 is used). This problem can also be eliminated by using a doubly-linked list. The drawback of this ADT is that one must use an additional memory location for each node. The standard trade-off in computer science once again appears — ease of use and some efficiency is gained at the expense of memory.

The node type for a doubly-linked list can be defined as follows:

```
TYPE   node = RECORD
                  leftlink : ptr;
                  info : INTEGER;
                  rightlink : ptr;
              END;
```

When using a doubly linked list, the *leftlink* of the head node is set to *NIL* as well as the *rightlink* of the tail node. It is also possible to have a header node with a doubly linked list and to make it circular.

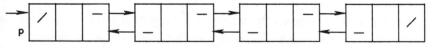

CHAPTER 7

STACKS

7.1 STACK STRUCTURE AND OPERATIONS

A **stack** is an ADT (abstract data structure) used for information storage in which data is inserted or removed from one "end," called the "top of the stack." A common (physical) example of the data structure *stack* is a stack of dishes in a cafeteria counter dish storage receptacle.

There are *three* common primitive stack operations.

1) **Push(x,s)** — *inserts* item x onto stack s (making x the new element at the top of the stack). (This operation is usually coded as a *procedure*.)

2) **Pop(s)** — *removes* the item at the top of the stack from stack s. (This operation is usually coded as a *function* and so the item removed from the stack is returned as the function value.)

3) **Peek(s)** — *copies* the value of the top of the stack but does *not* remove it from the stack s. (This operation is also usually coded as a *function* and so the item copied is returned

as the function value.) This function is sometimes called *Visit(s)* or *Stacktop(s)*.

To guarantee against errors, a fourth operation is commonly implemented:

4) **Empty(s)** — *checks* to see if there are any elements in stack *s*. (This operation is also usually coded as a *function* returning the boolean value of *true* if *s* is empty and *false* if there are elements in *s*.

NOTES ON STACK OPERATIONS:

a) Normally *Pop* or *Peek* cannot be performed on an empty stack, so the stack should be checked somehow before using either function. This can be done internally in *Pop* and *Peek* or it can be done before calling these functions if *Empty* is available.

b) Trying to *Pop* an empty stack induces an "underflow" error.

c) Trying to *Push* onto a "full" stack (if it does have any implementation-dependent limit) is called an "overflow" error.

d) Since *Push* and *Pop* both abbreviate to *P*, often *Stack* is used for *Push* (abbreviated *S*) and *Unstack* is used for *Pop* (abbreviated *U*).

7.2 USING STACKS

A stack can be most useful when it is necessary to remember the "last" unit of information stored. It is sometimes referred to as a LIFO structure (*L*ast *I*n, *F*irst *O*ut), a title that emphasizes the order in which the structure "remembers" items in it. The following examples will illustrate this. In all examples involving stacks, the assumption is that once an element has been popped off the stack, it cannot be pushed a second time back onto the stack.

(1) Given the input stream

A B C D E

and given the following sequence of stack operations (where S stands for Push [**S**tack], and U for Pop [**U**nstack})

S S U S S U S U U U

what is the output stream?

The operation of the stack will be given in detail for this first example:

INPUT STREAM	STACK OPERATION	: ← bottom	OUTPUT STREAM
A B C D E	S	⇒ A	
B C D E	S	⇒ A B	
C D E	U	⇒ A	B
C D E	S	⇒ A C	B
D E	S	⇒ A C D	B
E	U	⇒ A C	B D
E	S	⇒ A C E	B D
–	U	⇒ A C	B D E
	U	⇒ A	B E E C
	U	⇒ –	B D E C A

Thus the output stream is B D E C A.

(2) Given the input stream

ABCDE

and given the following OUTPUT streams, what is the command sequence that generated it?

a) BACED _____ SSUUSUSSUU

b) EDCAB _____ impossible output stream

Example 2b shows that even stacks have limitations. Although significant rearrangement of elements can take place, there are certain output combinations that are not possible, no matter how one arranges the order of pushes and pops. The problem arises in example 2b with item A. For E to be the first item out of the stack, it must have been the last one in, which implies that A is at the bottom of the stack. Thus, A must be the last element out.

Depending on the order of pushes and pops, one can change or even reverse the input order of data. Assume the input stream for both of the following examples is again:

ABCDE.

(3) Assume the command stream is:

SUSUSUSUSU.

The corresponding output would be

ABCDE.

(4) Assume the command stream is:

SSSSSUUUUU.

71

The corresponding output would be

E D C B A.

Because of these order properties, stacks can be useful in developing an algorithm to store information and then recall it in a certain *order*!

7.3 SAMPLE IMPLEMENTATION

7.3.1 ARRAY IMPLEMENTATION

Up to this point a stack has been presented merely as an ADT, without any consideration about how it is implemented in a given language or the many different ways it might be implemented. This section now addresses these implementation questions.

One way to implement a stack is to use the underlying data structure of an array. However, the same problems arise using arrays to implement a stack as occur when arrays are used to implement a linked list. The size of a stack is constantly changing, which makes it difficult to implement a stack exactly using an array, since arrays are *static* structures with pre-determined sizes.

Nevertheless, as was done with linked lists, an array can be declared of a size large enough to hold all the elements that would even be in a stack at one time. For each stack, a top-of-stack pointer is also needed that will serve as the (array) index to the top-of-stack element.

The following code implements a stack as a record, with one field being the array of elements, and the other being the top-of-stack pointer.

```
CONST   maxstack  =   100;

TYPE    stackitem  =   INTEGER;
        stack      =   RECORD
                          item : ARRAY[1..maxstack]
                              OF stackitem;
                          top : INTEGER
                       END;

VAR     s          :   stack:
```

7.3.2   CODING THE OPERATIONS

There are several ways of implementing stacks as arrays depending on whether one chooses to have the top-of-stack pointer point to the *last used* space or to the *next available* space, and whether the first used space has the subscript of *one* or the subscript of *maxstack*. The code below assumes (1) that the top-of-stack pointer points to the *last used* space and (2) that the first used space has the subscript of *one*.

The following code can easily be misused by combining operations together, thereby making the revised code much more difficult to read and reducing the analogy between the abstract data type (and its operations) and the implemented data structure. Newer languages such as Modula-2 and Ada allow data encapsulation so that the code is safe from such interference, but that does not prevent a programmer from writing the original code poorly.

Before using any stack *s*, it must be initialized by setting *s.top* equal to zero.

EMPTY

```
FUNCTION Empty(s:stack) : BOOLEAN;
BEGIN
```

```
        IF s.top = 0 THEN
            Empty := TRUE
        ELSE
            Empty := FALSE
    END; (* Empty *)
```

PUSH

```
    PROCEDURE  PUSH(VAR s:stack; x:stackitem);
    BEGIN
        IF s.top = maxstack THEN
            Writeln('stack overflow error')
        ELSE
            BEGIN
                s.top := s.top + 1;
                s.item[s.top] := x
            END (* else *)
    END;    (* Push *)
```

POP

```
    FUNCTION  POP(VAR s:stack) : stackitem;
    BEGIN
        IF Empty(s) THEN
            Writeln('stack underflow error')
        ELSE
            BEGIN
                Pop := s.item[s.top];
                s.top := s.top - 1;
            END (* else *)
    END;    (* Pop *)
```

PEEK

```
    FUNCTION Peek(s:stack) : stackitem;
    BEGIN
        IF Empty(s) THEN
            Writeln('stack underflow error')
        ELSE
            Peek := s.item[s.top]
    END; (* Peek *)
```

Notice that the only difference between Pop and Stacktop is that the top-of-stack pointer is changed in Pop.

7.3.3 POINTER IMPLEMENTATION

Stacks can be very simply implemented as linked lists. The top of the stack is merely the head node of the list. If the list is nil, the stack is empty. Elements are inserted and deleted from the head of the list. Using linked lists, a stack overflow will not normally occur since there is no array limit to worry about. However, when popping elements from the stack, care should be taken to dispose of unneeded nodes properly.

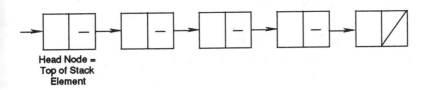

Head Node =
Top of Stack
Element

7.3.4 CODING SOME OPERATIONS

To show the similarity in the operations, even with using a different underlying data structure, the following examples are given.

DECLARATIONS OF DATA STRUCTURE

```
TYPE    stackitem  =  INTEGER;
        stack      =  ^node;
        node       =  RECORD
                          info : stackitem;
                          next : stack
                      END:


VAR     s          :  stack;
```

PUSH

```
PROCEDURE  Push(x:stackitem; VAR s:stack);
VAR p:stack;
BEGIN
    New(p);
    p^.info := x;
    p^.next := s;
    s := p
END;   (* Push *)
```

POP

```
FUNCTION  Pop(VAR s:stack) : stackitem;
VAR p:stack;
BEGIN
    IF Empty(s) THEN
        Writeln('stack underflow error')
    ELSE
        BEGIN
            Pop := s^.info;
            p := s;
            s := s^.next;
            Dispose(p)
        END (* else *)
END;   (* Pop *)
```

7.4 APPLICATIONS

Stacks are used in many ways, particularly when it is necessary to store information temporarily and then retrieve it in a reverse order. Two primary examples of this type of applications are (1) the evaluation of arithmetic expressions and (2) the analysis and removal of recursion. Since these topics deal with algorithms and applications, they are dealt with in Appendices C and D. The connection between stacks, arithmetic expressions and recursion will be merely sketched here.

Some hand calculators require that operators be entered last, after the operands. These are called "stack" or "RPN" (for Reverse Polish Notation) calculators. In other words, to add 3 and 5, first the 3 is entered, then the 5 and finally the + sign is pressed. In other words, 3 + 5 is equivalent to 3,5+ in RPN. A more complicated conversion is 3 + 4 × 5 which converts to 3, 4, 5, ×, +. Notice that in this second example, the order of the operators (+ and ×) are reversed. However, in a similar expression using parentheses, (3 + 4) × 5, the RPN expression keeps the operators in the original order, 3, 4, +, 5, ×. A program to convert between the standard arithmetic notation and RPN involves the use of a stack to store the operators. (Also see Appendix D.)

When a subprogram recursively calls itself, the computer does not duplicate the code. Rather, the values of all variables along with a return address are stored on stacks. During any use of the subprogram at any level of call, only the values that appear at the top of the stack on the various variable stacks are used. In this way, the subprogram "remembers" all the previous values of the variables it needs at any level. When it is desirable to eliminate recursion, a stack needs to be explicitly coded to keep track of the various values.

CHAPTER 8

QUEUES

8.1 QUEUE STRUCTURE AND OPERATIONS

A **queue** is a waiting line. This is a standard dictionary definition and the word is commonly used in British countries to designate any waiting line, not merely a computer science concept.

In computer science, a queue is an ADT (abstract data type) in which new data is inserted at one "end," called the *rear*, and stored data is removed from the other "end," called the *front*. Thus, in action it is identical to a waiting line that people experience while waiting for food in a cafeteria or for transportation at a terminal.

Since intermediate information in a queue *cannot* be reached, in action a queue is somewhat similar to a stack. However, whereas a queue is a FIFO (*first* in, first out) a stack is a LIFO (last in, first out) structure. Thus, unlike a stack, a queue does *not* (and cannot) change the order in which the elements are removed, relative to the order of their insertion.

There are *two* common primitive queue operations.

1) **Enqueue(x,q)** (often written Enq(x,q)) — *inserts* item *x* onto a queue *q* at its *rear*. (This operation is usually coded as a *procedure*.)

2) **Dequeue(q)** (often written Deq(q)) — *removes* the item at the front of queue (q). (This operation is usually coded as a *function* and so the item removed from the queue is returned as the function value.)

To guarantee against errors, a third operation is commonly implemented.

3) **Empty(q)** — *checks* to see if there are any elements in queue *q*. (This operation is also usually coded as a *function* returning the boolean value of *true* if *q* is empty and *false* if there are elements in *q*.)

Sometimes a fourth operation is found that is similar to the *Peek* operation on stacks. This function copies the value of the element at the front of the queue but does not remove it from the queue.

8.2 IMPLEMENTING QUEUES USING ARRAYS

8.2.1 THE UNDERLYING DATA STRUCTURE

Implementing the ADT of queues using the underlying data structure of an array involves the same problems as occurred with implementing stacks as arrays. Queues are dynamically changing in size, while arrays are static. But, similar to what was done with stacks, an array can be declared that is large enough to hold all items expected to be in the queue at any one time.

A queue needs *two* pointers: one indicating the index of the *front* and the other the index of the *rear*.

The following code implements a queue similar to the way a stack was implemented, i.e., via a record consisting of the storage array and two pointers.

```
CONST  maxqueue = 100;

TYPE    queueitem =   INTEGER;
        queue =       RECORD
                      item : ARRAY[1..maxqueue] OF
                                  queueitem;
                      front,rear : INTEGER;
                      END;

VAR q : queue;
```

8.2.2 PRESUPPOSITIONS

As with linked lists, certain presuppositions regarding the data structure and how it will be used need to be determined before coding the operations. In general, issues regarding the coding of queue operations require more thought and preliminary planning than did those regarding stack operations. As a result, a study of these issues provides an excellent example of some of the numerous (and frequently unexpected) problems that arise when dealing with more complicated data structures in applications programs.

There are three main issues for discussion:

Issue 1 — How should items be stored in the queue?

Issue 2 — What happens when the last space (i.e., the space with the greatest subscript value) in the underlying array has been filled?

Issue 3 — How is the test for an empty queue performed?

8.2.3 ISSUE 1: STORAGE OF ITEMS IN A QUEUE

There are two major options for storing items in a queue when the underlying data structure is an array.

(a) They can be always butted up to the front, so that the next items to be removed always is in array location 1. However, this option requires that all items in the queue be moved after each deletion, which can be highly time-consuming if there are numerous items and, thus, inefficient. However, this option would lead to a certain simplicity in coding the *Dequeue* function and in keeping track of the items in the queue.

(b) They can be left wherever they happen to be when inserted. This option complicates the computation of the *front* and *rear* pointers, but eliminates the time-consuming process of moving queue elements around. This option also makes it likely that after the queue has been used, an item will be inserted into the queue so that it is located in the last space of the underlying array, which leads to a discussion of the second issue.

8.2.4 ISSUE 2: FILLING THE UNDERLYING ARRAY

Even when a large array is used for the underlying data structure, after some use it is likely that a new element will be stored in the last space (i.e., the space with the largest subscript) in the array, but only a few elements will be "active" in the queue. To avoid wasting space and to be able to re-use the beginning of the array again, normally the array is thought of as "circular," in that after using the last space, the first space is then re-used (or "re-cycled"). However, this convention complicates the calculation of the pointers *rear* and *front*.

The choice of a circular array assumes the choice of the second option in resolving the first issue: namely that an item is not moved in the array after its insertion in the queue. However, these conventions may lead to the situation where *rear* < *front*. Thus, the code of the queue operations must take this into account. A circular array will be assumed in the discussion that follows, and it will also be assumed that when a Dequeue is performed, the *front* pointer is incremented by one and when an Enqueue is performed the *rear* pointer is incremented by one.

8.2.5   ISSUE 3: TESTING FOR AN EMPTY QUEUE

This issue actually leads to two new, but related, issues: (4) Can the array ever be completely filled with queue elements? and (5) Where should the *front* pointer actually point to? These new issues may seem ludicrous, but their importance will be seen in the discussion that follows. For now, assume that *front* and *rear* are the actual array indices of the first and last items stored in the queue, and that the array can be filled to capacity. There are several possible conditions for a queue to be empty that should be examined.

1) The condition *front* = *rear* would be an appropriate test for whether there is *one* element in the queue, but *not* whether the queue is empty.

x									

^   ^
F   R

2) The condition *front* > *rear* would work if the array was not considered to be circular. With a circular array, there could

be many elements in the array with the first element stored near the end of the array and the last element stored near the beginning, leading to *front > rear*.

Case 1: Natural Order — *front < rear* when non-empty.

	x	x	x	x	x	x	x		

      ^   ^
      F   R

Case 2: Wrap-around Order — *front > rear* when non-empty.

x	x						x	x	x

      ^   ^
      R   F

3) The condition *front = (rear* MOD maxqueue) + 1 would work if not for the fact that the array is circular and could be filled to the limit. Because of the circularity of the array, this same condition is true when the array is *full* (if every space is permitted to be used)!

Case 1: Almost empty queue.

BEFORE DELETION

	x								

      ^ ^
      F R

AFTER DELETION (*front* is increased by 1 and *front = rear* + 1)

      ^   ^
      R   F

Case 2: Almost full queue.

BEFORE INSERTION

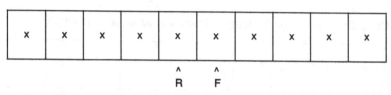

AFTER INSERTION (*rear* is increased by 1 and *front = rear* + 1)

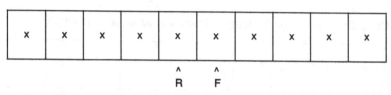

The dilemma raised by the third issue is usually resolved by making choices based on the two related issues mentioned: (4) Can the array ever be completely filled with queue elements? and (5) where should the *front* pointer actually point to?

In answer to (4), most implementations are coded so that one space is left "wasted" in the array. Thus, in an array of length *maxqueue* only *maxqueue – 1* elements can be stored. This eliminates the double meaning of the third possible condition.

Thus, the following conditions have these meanings:

	CONDITION	MEANING
1.	front = rear	One item in queue
2.	(rear MOD maxqueue)+1 = front	Empty queue
3.	(rear MOD maxqueue)+2 = front	Full queue

In answer to (5), because the conditions just listed seem non-intuitive, some implementations prefer to use the convention that *front* actually points to the "wasted" space in the array that is immediately *before* the first element. If this convention is chosen, the following conditions have these meanings.

	CONDITION	MEANING
1.	(front MOD maxqueue)+1 = rear	One item in queue
2.	rear = front	Empty queue
3.	(rear MOD maxqueue)+1 = front	Full queue

The last condition can be implemented so that when trying to *Enqueue* an item, *rear* is incremented first and then tested to see if it equals *front*. If it does, then overflow has occurred.

Some feel that keeping the pointers pointing to their "intuitive" elements is to be preferred even though the resulting conditions may not be clear. Others feel that keeping the conditions less complicated is to be preferred, even if the meaning of the *front* pointer is not exact. The choice can depend on the environment in which a queue is used. In either case, the questions raised by this (relatively simple) implementation provide excellent examples of the many issues that often need to be considered before coding operations related to data structures.

8.2.6   CODE FOR THE OPERATIONS

Based on the discussion above, *the following conventions have been chosen for the code that follows:*

1) Once inserted, an item is *not* moved in a queue.

2) The array is thought of as circular, i.e., after *q.item[maxqueue]* comes *q.item[1]*. Therefore, *front* (and *rear*) can also be increased to the next legal number by using the formula *front := front MOD maxqueue + 1*.

3) *q.front* is the index of the array element *immediately pre-*

85

ceding the first element in the queue. Therefore, if *q.front* equals *q.rear*, the queue is empty or overflow has occurred.

4) To enable a test for emptiness (and overflow), one element of the array is sacrificed as a queue element and used instead as a "dummy" element.

Before using any queue *q*, it must be initialized by setting *q.front* and *q.rear* both equal to zero.

EMPTY

```
FUNCTION Empty (q:queue: BOOLEAN;
BEGIN
        Empty := (q.front = q.rear)
END;   (* Empty *)
```

A longer way to code this function is to use the structure of the function Empty found in Section 7.3.2 and the condition (q.front = q.rear). However, the code above provides an alternate example, and shows the compactness that results by using a logical expression in an assignment statement.

ENQUEUE

```
PROCEDURE Enqueue (x:queueitem; VAR q:queue);
BEGIN
      BEGIN
          q.rear := q.rear MOD maxqueue + 1;
          IF q.rear = q.front THEN
              Writeln ('queue overflow error')
          ELSE
              q.item[q.rear] := x
END;   (* Enqueue *)
```

86

DEQUEUE

```
PROCEDURE Dequeue (VAR q:queue) : queueitem;
BEGIN
        IF Empty(q) THEN
            Writeln ('queue underflow error')
        ELSE
            BEGIN
                q.front := q.front MOD maxqueue + 1;
                Dequeue := q.item[q.front]
                END (* ELSE WITH q * )
END;   (* Function Remove *)
```

8.3   IMPLEMENTING QUEUES USING LINKED LISTS

Queues can also be implemented as linear linked lists. Often the choice is made that the head of the list is the front of the queue and the tail is the rear. Implementation is simplified if a second pointer to the rear of the list is also used, since insertions will constantly be made there, and it is more efficient to have a pointer always available to that part of the list. The head of the list is the "front" of the queue and is the point where elements are dequeued.

Certain implementation problems are also eliminated if the list has a header node, since otherwise coding is complicated when the queue is empty and when an item is inserted into an empty queue. However, this demands a function *Createqueue* that creates a new queue with merely a header node. The following diagram depicts a queue as a linked list with a header node.

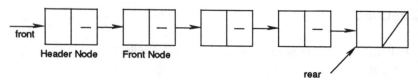

front | Header Node | Front Node | rear

The following definitions show how a queue can be implemented in Pascal using the underlying data structure of a linked list.

```
TYPE   queueitem  =  INTEGER;
       ptr        =  ^node;
       node       =  RECORD
                        info : queueitem;
                        next : ptr
                     END;
       queue      =  RECORD
                        front, rear : ptr
                     END;

VAR    q : queue;
```

Given the data structure definition, code for the various operations can now be written. Only one sample subprogram code is given, a linked list (pointer) version of the function *Dequeue*. Since linked lists are used, care must be taken with disposing of the formerly used node (as was done in the function Pop in Section 7.3.4), so the node space (no longer needed by the queue) can be re-used by the program.

```
FUNCTION Dequeue (VAR q:queue):queueitem;
VAR p:ptr;
BEGIN
        IF q.front = q.rear THEN
            Writeln ('queue underflow error')
        ELSE
            BEGIN
```

```
            p := q.front^.next;
            (* p now points to the real front node *)
            q.front^.next := p^.next;
            Dequeue := p^.info;
            Dispose(p)
        END (* IF..ELSE *)
END;    (* Dequeue *)
```

8.4 IMPLEMENTING QUEUES USING CIRCULAR LINKED LISTS

If a queue is implemented using a circular list, certain implementation details can be simplified further. Only one pointer is needed which can be used for both the enqueuing and dequeuing operations. This queue pointer points to the *rear of the queue*, but this rear (tail) node points to the head of the queue, since the list is circular. Thus, if *q* is a pointer to this queue structure, to enqueue an item the *InsAfter* procedure of Section 6.4.2 can be used and applied to *q*. To dequeue an item the *DelAfter* procedure of Section 6.4.3 can be used and applied to *q^.next*.

8.5 DEQUES

A **deque** (pronounced 'deck' as in a 'deck' of cards) is a *Double Ended Queue*. It is an ADT (abstract data type) in which insertions and deletions can be performed at either of two ends, usually called the *right* and the *left*.

Because of its configuration, a deque can function both as a stack (if insertions and deletions are done only at one end), or as a regular queue (by restricting insertions to one end and deletions to the other). If it functions as a queue, it can also act as a queue in either direction!

89

Deque operations are usually labeled as Right-Insert, Right-Delete, Left-Insert, Left-Delete, and Empty. They are modeled after the operations defined in stacks and queues. Implementation can be done via an array (as with a queue) or with a doubly-linked list. The coding of the various operations is similar to the codes given for the various implementations of other ADTs.

8.6   EVALUATION

The following is a brief comparison and evaluation of some of the many data structures seen thus far.

ARRAYS: Random access to any information cell.
If information is ordered, insertion (retaining the order) means shifting a lot of information.

STACKS: Sequential access.
One must pop the top-most cells of information off the stack to get to the desired cell. In many implementations, it is hard to "save" the popped information for re-use.
Cannot insert in the middle.

QUEUE: Sequential access.
One must dequeue to get to the desired cell of information. However, one can immediately enqueue the unneeded information to avoid loss.
Cannot insert in the middle immediately, without dequeuing and enqueueing in the correct order.

APPENDIX A

BINARY NOTATION

Binary notation, like decimal notation, is positional. Only two digits (bits) are possible in each place, 0 or 1. The place to the left of the binary point is called the *ones* place (as in decimal notation), but in binary notation it can also be indicated as the 2^0 place. The next position to the left is the *twos* (or 2^1) place. Next comes the *fours* place, then the *eights*, then the *sixteens*, etc., all labeled in successive powers of two.

Similarly, the places to the right of the binary point are labeled as negative powers of 2. The first place to the right of the binary point is the *halves* place, followed by the *quarters* place, followed by the *eighths* place, etc.

To translate from binary into decimal, a binary number should be expanded according to the appropriate (positional) power of two, and re-written in decimal notation. As an example, take 11010.101.

$$
\begin{aligned}
11010.101_2 &= 1 \times 2^4 + 1 \times 2^3 + 0 \times 2^2 + 1 \times 2^1 + 0 \times 2^0 \\
&\quad + 1 \times 2^{-1} + 0 \times 2^{-2} + 1 \times 2^{-3} \\
&= 1 \times 16 + 1 \times 8 + 0 \times 4 + 1 \times 2 + 0 \times 1 \\
&\quad + 1 \times (1/2) + 0 \times (1/4) + 1 \times (1/8) \\
&= 16 + 8 + 2 + 0.5 + 0.125 \\
&= 26.625_{10}
\end{aligned}
$$

To translate an *integer* from decimal into binary, the number should be repeatedly *divided* by 2 and the bits that form the *remainders* saved. This procedure stops when zero is reached as a quotient. These remainder bits, when read from last to first, form the binary equivalent. As examples, take 5 and 4.

Number	Remainder	Number	Remainder
2: 5	(none initially)	2: 4	(none initially)
2: 2	1	2: 2	0
2: 1	0	2: 1	0
0	1	0	1

Bits read last to first:

$5_{10} = 101_2$

Bits read last to first:

$4_{10} = 100_2$

To translate a *fraction* from decimal to binary, the number should be repeatedly *multiplied* by 2 and the bits that form the *overflow* (into the integer section left of the decimal point) saved. Once saved, the overflow bit is removed from the number as far as further calculations are concerned. This procedure stops when zero is reached as a product, or when it is obvious that the number is a repeating binary fraction, or when enough bits accurately have been achieved. These overflow bits, when read from first to last, form the binary equivalent. As examples, take 0.25 and 0.75.

Number	Overflow	Number	Overflow
2x .25	(none initially)	2x .75	(none initially)
0.50	0	1.50	1 (now remove)
2x 0.50		2x 0.50	
1.00	1 (now remove)	1.00	1 (now remove)
0.00		0.00	

Bits read last to first:

$0.25_{10} = 0.01_2$

Bits read first to last:

$0.75_{10} = 0.11_2$

APPENDIX B

SUBPROGRAM PARAMETER PASSING

When the major computer languages are analyzed, four principal methods can be identified that are used to communicate via (i.e., to "pass") parameters between a calling program and a subprogram. The standard names for these methods are:

    call by value
    call by reference (or "address")
    call by value-result (or "result")
    call by name (or "expression")

In some languages (e.g., Pascal, Ada), the programmer has the choice of determining the passing scheme for each parameter.

In other languages (e.g., FORTRAN, C), the user has no choice. The passing scheme is predetermined, but sometimes it is different for arrays than for scalars.

In *Pascal*, to use *call-by-reference*, the reserved word *VAR* is included before the parameter in the procedure or function parameter definition. If *VAR* is omitted, then the parameters are **call-by-value**. Call-by-value-result and call-by-name are not used.

In **FORTRAN**, there is no choice. The FORTRAN-77 definition seems to prescribe that all variables are passed as call-by-reference. However, in older versions of FORTRAN (e.g., FORTRAN IV, also called FORTRAN-66), scalar variables were usually passed as call-by-value-result and arrays were always call-by-reference. It is possible that this may still be true on some systems, at least when one specifies an older (e.g., FORTRAN-66) style of FORTRAN interpretation.

The four methods differ as follows:

In **Call by Value**, new (independent) memory locations are allocated in the subprogram and are initialized with **values** passed from the calling segment. Since the subprogram uses independent memory locations, the copied values may be changed without affecting the variables originally associated with them in the calling program. When the subprogram ends, the corresponding (actual) parameters in the calling segment are left **un**-changed.

In **Call by Reference (Address),** **no** new memory locations are allocated. Instead, a link is set up so that whenever a subprogram variable is referenced, the corresponding variable in the calling program is accessed and changed. Thus, both the calling segment and the subprogram share the **same** memory location. Often there may be two or more names for the same memory location, a phenomenon sometimes called "aliasing." Since both segments use the **same** memory location, it initially contains its value from the calling segment, and retains any changes introduced by the subprogram. What it passes is an **address** (i.e., a pointer), and not the value per se.

In *Call by Value-Result*, new memory locations are allocated in the subprogram and are initialized with *values* passed from the calling segment (so far, everything is the same as with call-by-value). Because it has independent memory locations, these values may be changed independently of the variables originally associated with them. However, when the subprogram ends, the corresponding actual parameters in the calling segment *are changed*!

In *Call by Name (Expression)*, the actual parameter is considered to be a character string, and a text replacement is performed in the subprogram for the formal parameter, wherever it occurs. As a result, an actual parameter may clash with a local variable because both are composed of the same characters and are considered to be one and the same. This method was once used in Algol-68 but is not in common use in major languages now.

EXAMPLE: CONFUSION

It can make a lot of difference in certain special cases how parameters are passed. The rules for the different passing schemes must be followed *brutally* by a human programmer when testing code by hand or else unconscious errors will occur resulting in answers that will differ from computer results. To show that problems may occur if a programmer is unclear as to which parameter passing scheme is used, and thus, unclear as to exactly what is happening between the calling segment and the subprogram, the following example is offered, written in a pseudo-language.

```
function icrazy(i, j, k) : integer
i = j + k
j = j + k
icrazy = i + j + k
k = j
```

```
        return
        end

— main program

        n = 5
        ivalue = icrazy(n, n, n)
        ivalue = ivalue + n
        write(ivalue)
        end
```

Depending on the type of calling method used, three different answers are possible:

CALL BY VALUE	= 30
CALL BY ADDRESS/REFERENCE	= 80
CALL BY VALUE-RESULT	= 35

In the *Value* and *Value-Result* methods, separate memory locations are allocated for each of *icrazy*'s variables, *i*, *j*, and *k*. Each variable ends with a value of 10 and the value of the function is 25. However, when *Value* is used, *n* in the main program is unchanged after the invocation of *icrazy* and remains 5. When *Value-Result* is used, *n* is changed to 10. Thus the output answers are 30 (call by value) and 35 (call by value result).

When call by *Address* is used, there is only one memory location between the main program parameter and the corresponding parameter in the procedure. Here, however, each parameter corresponds to the *same* variable in the main program, and so the same memory location has *four* different names (i.e., "aliases"), *i*, *j*, *k*, and *n*. When one variable's value changes, they all change values. Thus, at the first assignment statement in the function, *i* receives the value of 10 (and so do *j* and k). Then, at the second assignment statement, j receives the value of 20 (and so do i and k). Thus, *icrazy* receives the value of 60, and when the function is completed, *n* retains its changed value of 20. The final result is thus 80.

In this situation, call by *name* would yield the same results as *call by address*.

COMMENT

In the context of data structures, it can be important to know how a language passes parameters, because undesirable side effects can occur if one is unclear how the data is stored, how many copies exist, and when it changes. For example, type conversion can take place in FORTRAN if the actual parameters (in the calling segment) do not correspond in type with the formal parameters (declared in the subprogram header). This can lead to unexpected errors, such as truncation or even completely unrelated answers (depending on how the local compiler handles mis-matched parameter types).

In Pascal, if parameter arrays are not declared *VAR*, new memory is allocated whenever a subprogram is involved that can (needlessly) use up large amounts of memory. In extreme cases, in recursive routines, a run-time error may occur because of no more available memory.

In C, one has to "fool" the language in order to achieve a *call-by-address*, since it only uses call by value. This is normally done by passing a copy of the address of (i.e., pointer to) a variable, and then accessing (and changing) the variable's actual value through its pointer. Even though there are two pointers to the same memory location, when one changes the memory location pointed to, it remains changed, even though its pointer cannot be changed.

INDEX

HANDBOOK of
**MATHEMATICAL,
SCIENTIFIC, &
ENGINEERING**
FORMULAS, FUNCTIONS,
GRAPHS, TABLES,
& TRANSFORMS

R∯A RESEARCH & EDUCATION ASSOCIATION

A particularly useful reference for those in math, science, engineering and oth
technical fields. Includes the most-often used formulas, tables, transforms, functions, a
graphs which are needed as tools in solving problems. The entire field of special functio
is also covered. A large amount of scientific data which is often of interest to scienti
and engineers has been included.

Available at your local bookstore or order directly from us by sending in coupon below.

"The ESSENTIALS"
of Math & Science

Each book in the ESSENTIALS series offers all essential information of the fie it covers. It summarizes what every textbook in the particular field must include, a is designed to help students in preparing for exams and doing homework. T ESSENTIALS are excellent supplements to any class text.

The ESSENTIALS are complete and concise with quick access to need information. They serve as a handy reference source at all times. The ESSENTIA are prepared with REA's customary concern for high professional quality a student needs.

Available in the following titles:

Advanced Calculus I & II
Algebra & Trigonometry I & II
Anatomy & Physiology
Anthropology
Astronomy
Automatic Control Systems /
   Robotics I & II
Biology I & II
Boolean Algebra
Calculus I, II, & III
Chemistry
Complex Variables I & II
Computer Science I & II
Data Structures I & II
Differential Equations I & II
Electric Circuits I & II
Electromagnetics I & II

Electronics I & II
Electronic Communications I & II
Fluid Mechanics /
   Dynamics I & II
Fourier Analysis
Geometry I & II
Group Theory I & II
Heat Transfer I & II
LaPlace Transforms
Linear Algebra
Math for Computer Applications
Math for Engineers I & II
Math Made Nice-n-Easy Series
Mechanics I, II, & III
Microbiology
Modern Algebra
Molecular Structures of Life

Numerical Analysis I & I
Organic Chemistry I & I
Physical Chemistry I & I
Physics I & II
Pre-Calculus
Probability
Psychology I & II
Real Variables
Set Theory
Sociology
Statistics I & II
Strength of Materials &
   Mechanics of Solids I &
Thermodynamics I & II
Topology
Transport Phenomena I &
Vector Analysis

*If you would like more information about any of these books,
complete the coupon below and return it to us or visit your local bookstore.*

RESEARCH & EDUCATION ASSOCIATION
61 Ethel Road W. • Piscataway, New Jersey 08854
Phone: (732) 819-8880   **website: www.rea.com**

Please send me more information about your Math & Science Essentials books

Name _____

Address _____

City _____ State _____ Zip _____

"The ESSENTIALS"
of COMPUTER SCIENCE

Each book in the **Computer Science ESSENTIALS** series offers all essential information of the programming language and/or the subject it covers. It includes every important programming style, principle, concept and statement, and is designed to help students in preparing for exams and doing homework. The **Computer Science ESSENTIALS** are excellent supplements to any class text or course of study.

The **Computer Science ESSENTIALS** are complete and concise, with quick access to needed information. They also provide a handy reference source at all times. The **Computer Science ESSENTIALS** are prepared with REA's customary concern for high professional quality and student needs.

Available Titles Include:

BASIC
C Programming Language
C++ Programming Language
COBOL I
COBOL II
Data Structures I
Data Structures II
Discrete Stuctures
FORTRAN
PASCAL I
PASCAL II
PL / 1 Programming Language

*If you would like more information about any of these books,
complete the coupon below and return it to us or visit your local bookstore.*

REA's Test Preps
The Best in Test Preparation

- REA "Test Preps" are **far more** comprehensive than any other test preparation series
- Each book contains up to **eight** full-length practice tests based on the most recent exa
- **Every** type of question likely to be given on the exams is included
- Answers are accompanied by **full** and **detailed** explanations

REA has published over 60 Test Preparation volumes in several series. They include:

Advanced Placement Exams (APs)
Biology
Calculus AB & Calculus BC
Chemistry
Computer Science
English Language & Composition
English Literature & Composition
European History
Government & Politics
Physics
Psychology
Statistics
Spanish Language
United States History

College-Level Examination Program (CLEP)
Analyzing and Interpreting Literature
College Algebra
Freshman College Composition
General Examinations
General Examinations Review
History of the United States I
Human Growth and Development
Introductory Sociology
Principles of Marketing
Spanish

SAT II: Subject Tests
American History
Biology E/M
Chemistry
English Language Proficiency Test
French
German

SAT II: Subject Tests (cont'd)
Literature
Mathematics Level IC, IIC
Physics
Spanish
Writing

Graduate Record Exams (GREs)
Biology
Chemistry
Computer Science
Economics
Engineering
General
History
Literature in English
Mathematics
Physics
Psychology
Sociology

ACT - ACT Assessment

ASVAB - Armed Services Vocational Aptitude Battery

CBEST - California Basic Educational Skills Test

CDL - Commercial Driver License Exam

CLAST - College-Level Academic Skills Test

ELM - Entry Level Mathematics

ExCET - Exam for the Certification of Educators in Texas

FE (EIT) - Fundamentals of Engineering Exam

FE Review - Fundamentals of Engineering Review

GED - High School Equivalency Diploma Exam (U.S. & Cana⬛ editions)

GMAT - Graduate Management Admission Test

LSAT - Law School Admission ⬛

MAT - Miller Analogies Test

MCAT - Medical College Admis⬛ Test

MSAT - Multiple Subjects Assessment for Teachers

NJ HSPT- New Jersey High Sc⬛ Proficiency Test

PPST - Pre-Professional Skills T⬛

PRAXIS II/NTE - Core Battery

PSAT - Preliminary Scholastic Assessment Test

SAT I - Reasoning Test

SAT I - Quick Study & Review

TASP - Texas Academic Skills Program

TOEFL - Test of English as a Foreign Language

TOEIC - Test of English for International Communication

RESEARCH & EDUCATION ASSOCIATION
61 Ethel Road W. • Piscataway, New Jersey 08854
Phone: (732) 819-8880   **website: www.rea.com**

Please send me more information about your Test Prep books

Name _____

Address _____

City _____ State _____ Zip _____